GOD WORKS THROUGH DREAMS

Jenness Reid

www.worksoftrinity.com

Published by Works Of Trinity, LLC
Teaneck, New Jersey, 07666, U.S.A.
www.worksoftrinity.com

All scripture quotations are taken from The Holy Bible, King James Version (KJV) – *public domain*.

No part of this book may be reproduced or transmitted in any form or by any means; electronic or mechanical – including photocopying, recording, and information storage and retrieval systems; without written permission from the publisher. Send email to: permission@worksoftrinity.com.

God Works Through Dreams

Copyright © 2014 Jenness Reid, all rights reserved.
Commissioned by Jesus Christ

ISBN-13: 978-0-9831999-0-8 (paperback)
ISBN-13: 978-0-9831999-1-5 (electronic)
Library of Congress Control Number: 2014916533

Dedication

I dedicate this book to the works of The Trinity. This is my vision of God's children doing His works on earth through the power of God, Jesus Christ of Nazareth, and the Holy Ghost [Spirit]. The goal is to defeat Satan's kingdom on earth and free God's children from his interferences in their lives.

Disclaimer

Everything in this book relates to my dreams, dreams from a few relatives, how I see the fulfillment of the dreams in real life, my thoughts, and my opinions. The names of actual individuals and places have been changed for identity reasons.

This book is for educational purposes only, and only you are responsible if you choose to do anything based on what you read.

Jenness Reid

Contents

Guide to My Dream Writing 6

Preface 9

A Dreamer's Journey 19

New Life Dreams 24

Road to Recovery 31

Called to Be a Spiritual Warrior 60

Dreams of Death 79

Warnings of My Possible Death 98

Spiritual Incidents and Attacks 114

Sally's Struggles with Illness 134

Stand-alone Dreams 148

Work-related Dreams 169

An Outstanding Biblical Dream 185

A Look at Biblical Dreams 189

Summary 193

Bibliography 195

Acknowledgement

First, I give thanks to God for helping me through difficult times by giving me the amazing vision of complete wellness and the gift of His herb, through dreams.

Special thanks to my sister, Ruth, for her support during my difficult times and her dream contributions. Thanks to my daughter, Sonia, and niece, Petrona, for their dream contributions. Special thanks to my editors – Racquel, Patsy, and Sally, who edited the chapter about her.

Exceptional thanks to my sister, Catreen, for her dream contributions about the cure for my back problems.

Guide to My Dream Writing

To fully grasp the content of this book, it is important for me to explain how the writing of it came about. Upon awakening, I made it a habit to recall most of my dreams – mainly those that seemed significant. Sometimes I did not even have to think back because the dream was so vivid that it remained at the forefront of my mind when I awoke. In each entry, I record the events of the dream in detail to allow you to feel as though you are experiencing the dream right along with me.

Each dream includes a discussion of its fulfillment where I identify the characters and determine who, or what they represent. I am not always able to identify all the characters in the dream since its fulfillment can be in whole, or in part. I also try to determine why I had the dream and how it relates to my life. To identify the fulfillment of the dream, I consider the content, image, my thought process, and my feelings while having it. I sometimes make connection to other dreams, where I see relationships.

There always seems to be one or more aspects of my dreams that come true. A significant number of my dreams have already come true and have provided me with the basis for expected fulfillment of others. Some of my dreams did not have any current situation I could immediately relate them to, but later the situation developed. Some of my dreams have long-term fulfillment, up to five years; while others have short-term fulfillment, as short as ten minutes. The dream events unfold exactly, or partially, in relation to what occurs in real life. I also find that there can be a comical twist in the dream's fulfillment. Only when the dream is fulfilled does the relationship between it and awakening life becomes clear.

My dreams depict stories of health, pregnancy, work situations, death, matters of the soul, and spiritual attacks. The chapters are theme based, rather than chronological based, so that the reader can focus more on the dream stories. Some dreams are connected to each other. Where there are connections, I point them out. For example, I have seen where God gave me multiple dreams about trees to prepare me to receive and act on the dream my sister, Catreen, had about the cure for my back problem.

I do not consider myself an expert at interpreting dreams, but I am a master at identifying the fulfillment of my own dreams. I feel fortunate that I have witnessed many of my dreams being fulfilled and can share them with you, in your search to understand yours.

Preface

Dreaming is a part of life. God created us with an aptitude for dreams. Do you know the value of your dreams? Are your dreams warnings, revelations, or directions from God; are they from Satan, or, are they to be ignored? This book will spark a curiosity in you about your own dreams as I share my journey of how I learned to understand mine.

This book reflects the beginning of my spiritual journey. God started the journey with dreams. He took me from a place of ignorance to where I am in Him right now – the manager of the company He asked me to incorporate for Him. This book is for people who do not know much about God and wondered about His presence among us; people who may know about Him through Bible stories, but do not experience much of His presence; people who are just curious about His works in present time; and people who experience spiritual afflictions through dreams, created by those who practice spiritual wickedness.

Preface

You may not be close enough to God right now. But, do you know if He has a plan for you – that has been shown to you through dreams which you may be ignoring?

This book will leave you asking the question, *"Should I be paying attention to my dream?"* According to biblical prophecy, God will be pouring out His Spirit on everyone; your children will prophesy; old men will dream dreams; and young men will see visions (Joel 2:28-29). This book provides insights into such a day, as prophesied by the prophet Joel.

I must pause here to relate an incident which God used to confirm needed clarification of my writing about "limits" on Him and of dreams about deceased relatives. After I got feedback from a reviewer, God was faithful to confirm the changes needed to be made. I have been cautious about making updates without His permission, after He strongly discipline me when I was about to make changes in my other book, *God Has Gone Corporate*, based on feedback. For this update, He used a situation with the current U.S.A. president, Donald Trump, to indicate that there was an issue with how I expressed myself.

I had just replied to my reviewer, acknowledging the need for change, when my niece showed me a video clip of the president misspeaking about abortion. In his speech, he misspoke when he said, *"Right now, a number of state laws allow a baby to be born from his or her mother's womb in the ninth month. It is wrong. It has to change"* (Mcafee).

After President Trump spoke, I could feel the confusion of what he had said; obviously, he had misspoken. Babies are born at nine months according to God's law, not state laws. I knew that this was something to which I needed to pay attention. Although I had felt the confusion right away, it was while in the shower that The Holy Spirit pointed out to me that what happened to President Trump was like my writing error. I therefore, prayed fervently to God for days, before He assisted me in making the needed updates; that He is not limited and explain why He had to use my deceased relatives to get my attention. I know that some people might be quick to say it is of the devil since the devil does similar works. However, if you read on, you will understand the difference.

This book will also be helpful to Christians who know the Bible well, since it will re-enforce that God is not limited in what He can do, according to His word. It is us who limit what He wants to do through us. God gave me dreams about the upcoming death of my mother, which allowed me to warn her to prepare herself; and after she died, He gave me a dream to let me know that she is with the saints. Likewise, He gave my sister, Ruth, a dream of death, which was fulfilled for our sister, Catreen; and again, after Catreen died, He gave Ruth a dream indicating that Catreen would be with Jesus in Heaven. After re-assuring us that our deceased relatives' spirits are with Him, He then used them so that Ruth and I would pay special attention to our dreams. Otherwise, we would have dismissed our dreams, as we usually do. Once God got our attention, he stopped using them. If you get turned off about dreams of deceased relatives, at this point, then you will miss out on the very important beginnings of my journey with God, which is related to end-time works.

I am aware that the Bible advised us to join to all that are living, as a living dog is better than a dead lion; the dead does not know anything and has no say on anything that is done on earth (Ecclesiastic 9:4-6). This refers to the physical body. For the spirit, it is different. The Bible gives us the example of Saul, wrongly, reaching out to the dead for assistance with his problems. After the death of Samuel, because Saul was afraid of his enemies and he was not hearing from God, he went to a woman who had a familiar spirit and asked her to use it and bring up Samuel. This is a devilish mean of contacting the spirit of a deceased person, which he had condemned before. However, Saul was very disturbed by what he heard from Samuel and fell on the ground, feeling very weak (1 Samuel 28:3-20).

In a parable about the rich man and Lazarus, Jesus speaks about what happens to the spirit of the dead. He indicated that those who died in Him are at a place of comfort, while others are at a place of torment – Hell; people on either sides can see each other, but cannot cross the great gulf (divide) between them; according to the argument between Abraham and the rich man in Hell, Lazarus could have gone back to warn the rich man's brothers so that they could repent; however, Abraham pointed out that they have the living – Moses and other prophets to whom they should listen (Luke 16:19-31). In this parable, Jesus indicated that the spirit of the dead can see what is happening to the living. However, the living should be listening to each other.

In the book of John, Jesus addressed the power of God over the dead. He spoke of the Father raising the dead and giving them life, and He also can do the same to whom He pleases. Jesus spoke of the day when the dead will hear His voice. Further in this chapter, he made another connection with Moses; He told the people that although He came in His Father's name, they did not believe Him; they honored each other, but not Him Who came from God only; He said He would not complain about them to the Father, but Moses who they trusted, did; they did not believe Moses, otherwise they would have believed Jesus, because Moses wrote about Him; since they did not believe Moses' writing, Jesus questioned how they could believe His word (John 5:21, 5:25-29, 5:43-47).

I know that Jesus lead me to write about the issue that Moses had with people not believing his writing, although he wrote about Jesus. For me, my extraordinary experiences which Jesus asked me to write about, involve dreams of deceased relative which played a major role in me surviving the many attacks of Satan on my life. God has power over the deceased, which He exercised for me to accomplish His end-time mission, see Dream 4.7.

While we are not to seek after the dead and deal with them as we would with the living, God can use them for His works, if needed. In my case, God needed my sister and I to pay attention to our dreams, since we would have otherwise dismissed them.

Satan, the counterfeit of God, can cause confusion with dreams, since as in every other thing, he tries to capture souls by any mean. He can use deceased relatives to start and continue the process of capturing and enslaving you if he can. In case I do not recognize that my dream is from Satan, whenever I awake, I pass my dreams through the Holy Fire of my God (Adonai, the God of Abraham) to burn and destroy every plot and plan of the enemies against me, in dreams. I have had many encounters with Satan and his works, both in dreams and my awakening life. Being aware of the works of Satan, through dreams, does not deter me from acknowledging the works of God, through dreams.

My dreams are the foundation from which God started my development. The evil encounters I had in dreams were just training and preparation for overcoming spiritual wickedness. To be a soldier in the Army of The Lord, you must go through training. God used all the evil works of Satan in dreams and my awakening life to develop me into who He predestined me to be. So, it does not matter how Satan comes at me, through dreams or when I am awake; he is defeated. You, too, can defeat Satan, in dreams and in awakening life.

Dreams are more important than you think. Through a dream I experienced my first call of God – a call that requires me to destroy Satan's kingdom on earth and bring people to God. The call of God, through dreams, is not like the traditional *"altar call"* at church. Most people may not be attending church; therefore, God must find creative ways to bring people to Him.

My Qualification as A Dreamer

Religious people may think that I am not qualified to conduct business on God's behalf. However, God qualifies me from within, and not from without, as man would. After all, Jesus called the fishermen, Peter and Andrew, to be His disciples (Mathew 4:18-20) without them getting prior teaching. In their cases, Jesus Himself was their teacher – the same way God is dealing with me.

God was not interested in me interpreting dreams. He did not give me that gift. He just wanted me to pay attention to my dreams and, therefore, allowed most of my dreams to be fulfilled completely, or, in part. He first got me interested in noting my dreams, The Holy Spirit of God gave me a pregnancy dream about two of my co-workers to whom I was close. He gave me warning dreams of what was about to happen to me and revelation dreams of what was happening to me, spiritually. Later, I came to the realization He was using my dreams to prepare me for what He referred to in one of my dreams as *"God's mission."* God's mission proved to be the turning point of my life and formed the content of the book, *God's Mission: Spiritual Battles and Revelation of Anti-666.*

The Truth

Let the truth be told (Rodriguez). Her book inspired me to write the truth about my attitude towards Bible stories, before it got changed. I had just written the beginning sentence of this section as, *"Let the truth be known"* when The Holy Spirit of God corrected me in an unusual way. The moment I finished typing the sentence is the moment Kimbella Vanderhee said the words, *"truth be told"* (Vanderhee and Scott-Young). I immediately checked the title of the book I had just read and saw that I had incorrectly written the title as *"Let the truth be known"* instead of, *"Let the truth be told,"* which I had wanted to be my leading sentence. The Holy Spirit used an interview about a show which I often discouraged by daughter from watching, to correct me. I had objected to my daughter watching the show because its content is quite vulgar. She was watching it at the time I was working on my manuscript.

The truth is, *"God is seeking to save EVERYONE"* through His Son, Jesus Christ; even the most vulgar of sinners. The other truth is that I never sought to study the Bible deeply. I did some reading and when I realized I was not seeing The Holy Spirit of God working with and through people as in Bible stories, I thought, *"Good for them, but what about us?"* I still maintained my love for God in my heart but kept wondering why He was not with us as He was with men like David, Moses, Joshua, and Samuel.

Little did I know, God had a plan for me – a plan involving dreams. Do you know if God has a plan for you in which He might be preparing you through dreams?

Chapter 1
A Dreamer's Journey

According to Merriam-Webster ("dream"), dream is *"a series of thoughts, images, or emotions occurring during sleep."* It doesn't speak of our awakening language (Delaney). Hence, some of us might not pay any attention to our dreams. However, some dreams have such an impact on you they have you wondering about their meanings.

Although it is natural for all of us to dream, for some of us dreaming is a gift from God that allows Him to communicate with us in an environment away from the many distractions we encounter during the day. I experienced my gift of dreaming when I was just four years old. My first unforgettable dreamer's experience was just a taste of what my future journey as a dreamer would involve. Here is the dream when I was four years old.

I am outside my mother's house in Jamaica, on a flat grassy piece of land, surrounded by sparsely distributed fruit trees and flowers. The house is almost diagonally across the old Presbyterian Church. I am standing below a window and looking in the direction of the church.

The sun is very big and bright. To my amazement, I see Jesus comes out of the sun. He resembles a picture my mom has, representing Him, in her living room – a handsome white guy with long hair and beard.

Jesus comes and stands right in front of me. He tells me something in a firm yet tender voice. I feel strong and wonderful in His presence. He leaves me feeling elated, important, and happy.

I can easily recollect the ambiance surrounding Jesus' presence. However, I simply cannot remember what He said to me no matter how hard I try. Perhaps His message was not meant to be revealed to me at that time. At four years old, to experience my gift of dreaming might have been easy, but to understand it was a challenge. Looking back, I think Jesus was probably telling me one day I would carry out His work on earth. This is hardly a message a four-year-old would have been able to fathom or comprehend; hence, my work and life changing events did not take place until adulthood.

Jesus was faithful in allowing me to connect this dream to my adult life experiences. On April 8, 2012, I attended Easter Sunday service at the church in this dream and did a presentation on the books I was writing. I told this dream and two other dreams. At the end of the service, someone in the congregation told me he noticed I had braided the *"Star of David"* at the back of my head. He later showed me the *"Prayer of David"* and explained that the circle around the star was the sun. I had my hair braided to represent God's business logo, which has a six-sided star within double circles. Jesus used a member of the congregation to confirm my writing of Him being the red star in the logo. He also allowed me to connect God's business logo to this dream.

Dreaming Transition from Childhood to Adulthood

After an accident in March of 2002, my childhood gift of dreaming was resurrected. My dream patterns changed drastically. In that, most of them no longer escaped my memory when I awoke, but remained vividly etched in my mind, weeks later. I started to write about them in a dream diary.

After starting my dream diary, I began consulting dream books to understand what these visions meant, but their interpretations did not accurately explain my dreams. The contradictions and inconsistencies in explaining my dreams were confusing. In one dream book, a triangle foretells separation from friends, and love affairs that will terminate in disagreement (Miller). In another dream book, a triangle foretells new beneficial conditions and opportunities, which you would do well to exploit (Robinson and Gorbett). After reading many dream books, I remained confused.

Before the accident, I relied on my Jamaican cultural interpretation of dreams. I was born in rural Jamaica. I lived there until I was 25 years old before migrating to America. In my Caribbean culture, dream meanings were always interpreted with input from friends and families. The importance of symbols in dreams is embedded in the Jamaican culture.

I learned about dreams from the elders in my family and their insights have been implanted in my memory. Their way of interpreting dreams survived throughout history but has lost its connection to the origin. For example, dreaming about fire indicates confusion; new shoes indicate a new lover; wedding indicates funeral; and new house indicates death (Tortello). With my new pattern of dreams, I had to disregard the Jamaican cultural interpretations and search for answers elsewhere.

God Used Dream in My Recovery

I realized God was using dreams to direct my life and to reassure me He was with me throughout my spiritual battles; although the assaults were initially masked as *"purely"* back problems.

Because of the grief caused by car collision, God used it as the perfect opportunity to step in to guide my life. I spent more time focusing on my complete recovery, based on the promise of God, through one of my dreams. The usual distractions of the busy workday were secondary to this.

There are many dreams where it was clear to me God was directing my spiritual recovery process; though initially I thought I was recuperating solely from a physical trauma. Many of my dreams have to do with responses from God, after praying about my concerns.

Chapter 2
New Life Dreams

My identity as a dreamer was created after I had my first pregnancy dream about two co-workers. This was the beginning of a new me. I had a few pregnancy dreams that came in different forms and got fulfilled by different means. The meaning of pregnancy fulfillment can be a physical pregnancy, adoption of a child, or, in my case, a symbol of my birth as an insightful dreamer.

(Dream 2.1, Pregnant Co-workers, 3/25/2003, Jenness)

I am sitting in my cubicle at work when my co-worker and friend, Sadie, comes to me and sits down. She tells me she is pregnant.

I then notice our supervisor, Tara, who is of the same age as Sadie, sitting some distance behind us. I somehow realize that she too is pregnant. I am thinking, "This is interesting because they each have a son the same age and once again would have another child of the same age."

Sadie got pregnant six months after I had this dream and Tara got pregnant a month after Sadie. The fulfillment of this dream was a clear sign that my gift of dreaming had been birthed; like the way an infant enters the real world for the first time.

The next day after this dream, I decided to tell Sadie about it. She was a little surprised. She said she and her husband were debating about having another child before she got older, but she wasn't pregnant. She was thirty-five years old at the time. I told her "now" would be the time to get pregnant if she really wanted another child. At that point I did not mention Tara was also pregnant in the dream.

Six months later, Sadie sat down in my cubicle and said she had something to tell me. I was thinking I would be hearing some rumors. But, as it turned out, she announced she was pregnant. I was pleased to hear that so far, a part of my dream came true.

I then told Sadie that within the same dream of her being pregnant I had realized Tara was also pregnant. We both agreed that would be very, very interesting if it were to happen. We decided to watch Tara for signs of pregnancy.

Tara was out sick for one week. Sadie and I really wondered about that and grew suspicious that my dream might be confirmed as true. However, when she returned to work it seemed as if she was recovering from a cold. Sadie and I continued to look for signs of pregnancy, anyway. Soon we noticed a slight belly bulge and an unusual change in her choice of clothing.

At a staff meeting, Tara announced she was in fact pregnant, but it was no surprise to Sadie and me. It was then Sadie and I announced to our group that long ago, I had dreamt she and Tara were pregnant. All my group members were impressed because they were already aware I had dreamt about Sadie's pregnancy six months before it happened. It was interesting Tara's pregnancy was a month behind Sadie's. According to the dream, she was sitting further behind Sadie.

In July of 2004 Sadie had a baby boy. In September of 2004 Tara had a baby boy. The dream and pregnancy forged a relationship between Sadie and Tara. I felt happy to be the dreamer of "new beginnings," not knowing that I was creating my own "new beginning" in the process.

(Dream 2.2, Tiny Lizard Jumps on Me, 04/14/2004, Jenness)

I am sitting on my couch at home. I see a tiny Polly lizard. It jumps at me. I know it does not mean any harm, but I am frightened. I know it is successful in landing on me.

This dream was fulfilled in the traditional way. According to the Jamaican traditional interpretation, if a lizard jumps on you, someone close to you would get pregnant. My niece, Gloria, got pregnant after this dream.

(Dream 2.3, Tiny Lizard in A Jar, 08/4/2004, Jenness)

I am sitting in my couch at home. I see the same tiny Polly lizard I dreamt about previously. This time it is in a big glass jar. It is just walking around on the inside of the jar.

I began to get worried because my two daughters were spending summer vacation with their grandparents in Jamaica. I called my daughters and warned them about becoming pregnant. I told the dreams to my sisters and they too called to warn my daughters.

Later I heard that my niece, Gloria, was pregnant. She had her baby in early July 2005. My dream occurred exactly when she was in the early stages of pregnancy.

(Dream 2.4, Second Pregnancy Dream About Tara, 10/28/2005, Jenness)

I am at a house which is under construction, judging from the debris inside. I see many small lizards between the glasses of one window. I am wondering how to get rid of them.

While trying to figure how to get rid of the lizards, my attention is drawn to my supervisor, Tara. She is sitting down. She has her blouse drawn up above her belly. I can see her belly clearly. I notice a slight bulge in her belly. I start to wonder, "Is she pregnant again?"

This dream reminded me of the ones I had about the tiny Polly lizard, which was fulfilled with my niece getting pregnant (Dream 2.2 & Dream 2.3). With this similarity, I wondered if Tara was pregnant again. In 2003, I successfully dreamt about her previous pregnancy (Dream 2.1).

Shortly after leaving my group, Tara was out sick for about two weeks. However, I did not see any signs of pregnancy after she returned to work. If she was pregnant and lost the baby, I would never know. The dream had indication of losing the baby, like my thoughts of getting rid of the lizards.

(Dream 2.5, Follow Up to Tara's Second Pregnancy Dream, 11/12/1005, Jenness)

I am in a conference room at work, sitting with my supervisor, Tara, two female co-workers, Sally and Jan, and a male co-worker, Reenan, from our group. We know Tara wants to tell us something but is finding it very difficult to do so. I somehow know it is about her pregnancy.

After sitting there for a while with nothing being said by anyone, I say to Tara, "Tara, don't worry about it, I already dreamt you are pregnant." She is relieved to hear that and starts talking.

This dream was a follow-up to the previous dream suggesting Tara might have been pregnant (Dream 2.4). I had this dream two weeks after the second pregnancy dream about her. Although she had been out sick for a while there was no evidence of her being pregnant.

(Dream 2.6, Adoption Pregnancy, 1/20/2006, Jenness)

I am in a room with my sister, Ruth. My grand-niece, Sasah, comes into the room. Her parents, John and Liz, follow in. I can tell both the parents are angry with her. Sasah is very upset. She says, "I don't know why they won't let me work." She walks out of the room.

Ruth and I sit down with John and Liz, to talk. I look at Liz and see her belly and breast are much larger. I am shocked. I say, "Liz, are you pregnant?" She is very hesitant in replying. I am thinking it is a bad situation to be in when they have so much expense.

This dream was fulfilled in a relative way. Although Liz wasn't pregnant as in the dream, in reality she and John later announced to Ruth and me that they adopted a girl.

****

A dreamer's entrance into the realm of the dream world does not always start with a string of birth related dreams. However, for me, these symbolic dreams illustrated the beginning of my dreamer's journey. Although you are given the gift of dreaming, you must do some interpretation to come to the realization that the dreaming gift has been bestowed upon you.

Physical pregnancy, adoption, or thoughts of pregnancy all represented new beginnings in different ways. It is important to see that these symbols can take on different forms but represent the same idea. A new life starts as a dream and from this new perspective and understanding, all dreams continue to grow.

Chapter 3

Road to Recovery

In unbelievable ways, God is constantly directing my health situation, through dreams, as would a medical doctor. This chapter includes dreams God has given me to help me through my recovery from what I thought was just back problems.

After failing to find a possible medical or scientific means of cure for my back problem, I began to put all my hope in God for Him to cure me by His means. I let go of worldly methods and used His instead. I strengthened my trust, faith, and determination in my spiritual relationship with God. He then revealed the gift of His herb. This gift was God's way of telling me I would get better.

God's gift eased the pain of relentless back problems that caused me to have many sleepless nights, miss out on fun activities, avoid going to church due to aggravation on uncomfortable chairs or benches, and even shy away from family embraces because of back pains.

I foolishly tried every method before I tried God's method. I had done physical therapy; spent a lot of money on massage therapy; I was under the constant care of a chiropractor; tried a number of physical trainers to scope out the right kind of exercises I needed for speedy recovery; tried book instructions on stretching exercises for back problems; tried special exercises that targeted trigger points in the body; and bought numerous types of exercise equipment such as elastic bands, expensive state-of-the-art exercise machine that utilizes vibration technology, step aerobics, foot pedals, trigger point massager, hand held massager, multiple hot water bottles, ice packs, and exercise videos, all in an effort to speed up the recovery process. All these desperate measures produced a roller coaster type of recovery in which I seemed to get a little relief, only to get aggravated later.

After chasing after practically every natural means of healing back problems I heard of and seeing them fail one after the other, I completely surrendered control of my recovery to God. I erroneously thought God would use one of these natural means I pursued to heal me. It was only after I allowed God to intervene through my dreams that I was able to start my journey on the path to recovery.

Because of my health-related dreams, I held on to God's promise to heal me. The dreams of the mind that got fulfilled in the physical body bolstered my spiritual strength and confidence in God. The first step is to realize that God can heal you, and then understand how He communicates His healing instructions through dreams.

(Dream 3.1, Feeling Better, 2/12/2003, Jenness)

I am outside my house sitting with my daughter, Sonia, at the side of the driveway. Work on the house is finished. It is extended at the back. Somehow, I realize my husband is no longer living here.

Sonia and I are just relaxing. My body feels good all over. It has a very strong healthy feeling of well-being. It reminds me of the feeling I used to experience after doing a good workout in aerobics class, at the gym.

While Sonia and I are sitting, my older daughter, Kristal, comes walking towards us with two men. I somehow know I am a friend of one of them and they are twins. The stature of the taller man reminds me of a family friend named, Ronald.

I awoke in dismay to find the feeling of well-being had vanished. However, because of this dream, I finally give into my husband's persistent requests for a major home improvement. The dream indicated I would be healed after the house was finished. I thought because I was not well, it was not the best time for such a massive project. In this dream, God revealed to me I would be completely healed after re-modeling work on my house was finished and my husband was gone.

I did not see at the time that the rebuilding and remodeling work done to our home was symbolic of the rebuilding and foundational strengthening God was currently working on in my life. He gave me a taste of His promise of healing to keep me going when times get rough. I reminisced on this dream during the many difficult times I faced on this journey. It gave me such a strong determination to get well. It never allowed me to feel that I should give up hope, even when I encountered failure.

I knew God was in control of my recovery. I trusted Him to reveal His ways to me. But as it turned out, His way was no sudden miracle either; contrary to my expectations. However, I knew God will keep such a Divine promise. I was praying every night and expected that one night I would get up feeling totally better. God's plan for me, however, was to bring people to Him through my experiences, not for me to be healed overnight. This was revealed to me in two other dreams (Dream 4.5; 4.6).

(Dream 3.2, How I Got Over, 2/30/2005, Jenness)

I find myself in very heavy traffic. It seems as if I am going to work. I decide to take an alternate route to avoid some of the traffic. In front of me I see a sign with the name, "Bartow," and the directional arrow. According to how the directional arrow of the road is shaped, I figure I can take that road and then get back onto the main road. I make a right turn onto Bartow.

I suddenly come across a very large body of water in front of me, as I turn to the right. The water is blue and very clear – much like what you see in the Caribbean. I am in awe!!!

The road continues a little further until it ends in the body of water. The right of the road has a low wall and the body of water comes up against it. There is a road to the left which I figure is the one I will have to take to get back on the main road.

There is a black man in front of me, as I stop to admire the huge body of water. The water is very close to my right; only a concrete barrier separates it from me. *Somehow, I am not in the vehicle although I am supposed to be driving. I say to the man in front of me, "This must be the ocean." Suddenly, the water on the right rises and washes over me. It gives me a shocking thrill and a cold feeling of being washed clean.*

With the thrill of this dream, I woke up suddenly, singing, "How I got over, how I got over, my soul looks back and wonders how I got over."

God had given me a song to encourage me and to reveal to me I would get over my troubles. This was a song familiar to me. For more than fifteen minutes after waking up I just couldn't stop singing the song, over and over in my mind. It gave me such a victorious feeling. I knew somehow, I would overcome physical back problems. I had been hanging on to God's promise of healing, since I had the dream about feeling better (Dream 3.1). God wanted me to keep hanging on to that promise.

After this dream, I obtained the song. I refer to it as "*my dream song.*" It gave me hope and increased determination whenever I listened to it.

(Dream 3.3, Unusual Tree, 5/30/2006, Jenness)

My sister, Ruth, and I are at Uncle Greg's house. We are at a spot where a fruit tree, called hog berry, is located. It bears very small, green, round fruits. I find myself with three of them in my hand. Ruth and I are not sure what kind of fruit it is because they are far bigger than hog berries. We are trying to figure out what kind of fruit we have when I look across to my other uncle's land, which is adjoining.

I see my cousin, Betty, and her husband, playing together. I say to Ruth, "Let us go and ask Betty and John." We walk over to them and I ask them if they can tell us what kind of fruit we have. Betty tells us a name, but I know she is wrong.

I then notice an unusual tree. It is two trees in one. The tree is short but there are two distinct roots with the smaller one having a brighter color than the other. The smaller root is entwining the larger one up to where the branches start. I gaze in amazement from the root of the tree to the branches. Where the branches separate, I can see that the smaller root belongs to an ackee tree and the other is a tamarind tree. The ackee tree has a few ackees on it. I turn to Betty and John and say, "You can videotape this and sell it. You can make a lot of money. This is very unusual."

This dream was preparing me to accept my sister, Catreen's, dream about the cure for my back problems

(Dream 3.7). The three trees in the dream represented the three trees from which I would get the fruits that formulated God's herb, from Catreen's dream. The entwinement of the trees relates to the fact that I had to combine the fruits from the trees to make God's herb.

(Dream 3.4, Blossoming Trees, 6/13/2006, Jenness)

I am at my mother's house. I am at a spot where a mango tree is located at a fence bordering our neighbor, Miss Sally. I notice two very tall trees. They are very close together, a little separated at the root, but start touching a little further up. When I look way up to the branches, I see that both trees are very heavily laden with petals. They are ready to start bearing fruits. My sister, Ruth, joins me. I show her the trees and point out how they are heavily laden with petals. I tell her, "This is what the other dream with the two trees is about."

Ruth leaves; after this a co-worker, Jay, comes along and notices the trees. After seeing how laden they are with petals, he shakes the trees. A small number of petals falls off. I bounce him with my hip and tell him," Those are my trees. Leave them."

This dream was yet another revelation about God's herb. The entwinement of the trees was related to the fact that I had to combine the fruits from the trees to make the herb. The time for the herb revelation to my sister, Catreen, was getting closer at that point. The flowering of the trees was an indication of that.

(Dream 3.5, The Fence, 8/1/2006, Jenness)

I am at a place where there are a lot of people; some are my co-workers. One of my co-workers, Don, is playing table tennis with my daughter. I watch them for a while, and then I notice an ackee tree. I say, "I would like to see this."

From a distance, it seems as if some of the ackees on the tree are opened. I go closer. When I can see more clearly, I think, "There are a lot of opened ones."

As I get closer to the ackee trees, I notice some tamarind trees. I also notice some green healthy-looking mango trees, but these do not have any fruits yet. As I get very close, I notice a fence around the property where the trees are located. I think to myself, "This is Castle Land. The fence is to keep out people."

This was also yet another dream about ackee tree to keep me focused on the main ingredient of God's herb. As it turned out, the dream about God's herb was close in coming.

(Dream 3.6, Jenness Will Get Better, 8/16/2006, Catreen)

I am in my mother's room, talking to her. It is as if I went to visit her. The children are there also. She says to me, "You always want me to say I appreciate what you do, but don't worry. I am proud of you." She then admires the children, saying how they are all grown up, especially Anna.

She says, "I want you to know that I am very happy. I saw Evelyn and she is all right. Ruth and Jenness will be all right." I tell her Jenness is still suffering from back problems. She says, "Jenness has pain in her back because she was lifting heavy stuff." I said, "No. It is because of the car accident." She says, "Tell Jenness she will get better."

God chose my sister, Catreen, to be the messenger of my cure before she died. It really uplifted her spirit to have such a dream. She already knew I was having real dreams – dreams that were fulfilled. She was happy to start having the same kind of experience. After this dream, she got very excited and called to tell me.

Before my mother died, she was aware of the ongoing problems I had with my back, after a car accident. She was constantly inquiring as to how I was recovering from it. It was interesting that my mother was denying my back problem was due to the car accident I had. Instead, she pointed to something else. As it was revealed later, the accident and the resulting back problems were distractions for spiritually inflicted harms. This is written about in the book, *God's Mission: Spiritual Battles and Revelation of Anti-666*.

(Dream 3.7, The Cure for Jenness, 8/21/2006, Catreen)

I am at my mother's house with her. I know she has a lot of things to discuss with me. We walk to where her tomb is located and she shows the tombs and tells me they need weeding out. She shows me a plant at the fence, bordering her neighbor's property. It is close to the tombs.

I say to her, "It is just a plant." The leaves looked familiar to me. They are soft and have cut edges. She says, "Don't forget this special plant. Boil it with thyme leaf and the core of the apple to make tea. Jenness should drink it to strengthen her back. You should also drink it." She then takes me to where the apple tree is located. It looks like American apple, green and red.

I pick one of the apples and start eating it. She says, "Use the core of the apple to boil with the other plant leaves. Don't forget the plant by the fence. Ronald is envious. Remember now. Don't forget what I told you."

I knew my mother made it to Heaven after she died. God chose her to give my sister, Catreen, the message of the cure for my illness, before she too died. This was the most awesome dream I heard since it was about my cure.

Catreen called me and told me the dream. We were excited more than ever. She also called my sister, Ruth, and told her the dream. Ruth immediately contacted my brother, Carl, who was in Jamaica and told him the dream. She asked him to go and check out the areas where our mother showed Catreen the plants.

Based on the dream, Carl went and looked at the location for the apple and other trees. He was able to identify all plants. He found out the plant represented by apple, was used in olden days to cure bruises and swelling from injuries.

Another plant was a vegetable and well known for purging the blood.

Carl was able to send us a small sample of the tea. Although it was a small amount, I felt a refreshing feeling going throughout my body as I drank it. I later found my muscles started to lose some of its tightness. I got very excited after that.

Catreen and I started having a lot of discussions back and forth. We finally decided we would go to Jamaica, so I could complete my healing process. We booked our flights to go down the week of Thanksgiving. Unfortunately, Catreen died two weeks before we were scheduled to go. She died in good spirit – feeling good about herself, because of the honor such a wonderful dream brought her. However, this was a big blow to me. I felt she had left me to carry on the task of making my medicine from scratch, on my own. I pursued the cure of my back problems not merely for myself, but for both of us.

I felt, finally God had shown me His way of fulfilling His promise of wellness that was indicated in another dream (Dream 3.1). Catreen's dream of the cure did not take place until I was tired and weary of trying to do it my way and finally told God I was beaten, broke, and was leaving it all up to Him to perform His miracle. What was so impressive about this dream was that God waited until my mother died so He could use her to deliver the cure. I learned the lesson that, we just never know how God will do His work. He can use those who died and made to a place of rest, in Him, to further His work on earth.

(Dream 3.8, Special Vitamin, 11/25/2006, Jenness)

I find myself with a bottle of vitamins in my hand. I am trying to read the label. The brand name starts with the letter "A" but I cannot clearly figure out the rest of the letters. I look to see the ingredients; I can clearly see calcium and magnesium.

On November 30, 2006, I went to my chiropractor after not visiting him for a while. I felt that since my muscles started to relax because of taking God's herb (Dream 3.7), he would be better able to help with his usual adjustments and muscle work.

I asked the chiropractor how to measure the effect of a medicine other than by how your body felt. He told me pH measurement of the urine or saliva could possibly indicate if a medicine was helping to get the body into the right pH range, either too acidic or too alkaline.

The week before this dream, on November 18, 2006, I had a dream about a co-worker accusing me of not measuring the pH. I made the connection of that dream to what the chiropractor told me.

I visited a website and ordered pH stick for testing my urine. I noticed they also sold vitamins and minerals. Later, I went back to check if they had any calcium and magnesium mixture. I found the brand name "Alkaline Blue" for calcium and magnesium. The brand name starts with "A" as the vitamin in this dream. It was interesting that the write up about the value of their calcium and magnesium was to remove excess acid from the muscle. They said the body would store acid in the muscle when it could not eliminate all through the kidney or by sweating.

I took Alkaline Blue for a while but stopped after I noticed my body reacted negatively to it. While reviewing the manuscript for this book, I visited the website where I bought this vitamin and found that they no longer sell it. This dream was from God's enemy to counteract the effect of His herb.

(Dream 3.9, Chased by a Cow, 11/25/2006, Jenness)

I am at the border of my mother's house and the Presbyterian Church when I see my cousin, Denton. He is walking away from me as I am talking to him. I say to him, "I know how you are feeling because we are both suffering from the same problem." I am referring to my back and muscle problems.

After he goes out of sight I see a cow coming towards me. I know the cow likes me, but I don't want to be bothered with her. I start running away from her.

I see a tree and started thinking of climbing it to get away from the cow. I stop to examine the tree and see that black ants weakened the root and branches. I can see the dark areas where the ants are residing. I decide it is too risky to climb the tree since it looks too weak. While I am contemplating if I should climb the tree, I realize the cow has stopped and is watching me. After I decide not to climb the tree the cow disappears.

A man replaces the cow. I know he is madly in love with me. I start running away from him and he starts chasing me. As I run, I am threatening him, telling him I will karate him if he doesn't leave me alone. That doesn't stop him.

I misinterpreted this dream as confirmation I need to take calcium for my bones since cow represented milk and milk is a very popular source of calcium. This dream occurred the same night as the "Special Vitamin" dream with the bottle having calcium and magnesium written on it (Dream 3.9). At the time of this dream, I was taking God's herb (Dream 3.7) – a special mix of fruits and vegetable I put together for my back problem. I erroneously concluded the two dreams were telling me to take calcium and magnesium along with the herb. As it turned out, the special calcium and magnesium vitamin I found caused an adverse reaction.

When I told this dream to my sister, Ruth, she immediately concluded the man chasing me was the devil. After all, the devil also communicates through dreams and as it turned out, the special vitamin I found was to counteract my progress with God's herb. As the black ants eating away at the tree indicated, the devil was seeking to destroy the works of God, through dreams. From my multiple dreams experiences, I have learned to pray about my dreams and pass them through the Holy Fire of my God (Adonai – the God of Abraham) to destroy any plot and plan of the enemies against me, in dreams.

(Dream 3.10, I Get Rid of Ants, 12/11/2006, Jenness)

I am in the community where I grew up. I am across the street from the Parish tank. I see Hanna, a cousin, and realize she is living a little above where I am standing. I say to her, "I didn't know you are living up here." She replies, "Yes. Petra is living with me." I know she is referring to my sister, Petra.

After a while I realize I am standing in a nest of small black ants. There aren't many. Some are on my feet. I start to remove those on and around my feet. After brushing away the ants for a while, I walk away without any on me.

I go to sit under a huge tree with very large roots. The roots can be seen because the road is cut right against the tree. There are a few ladies from the area sitting under the tree. One of them is my cousin, Cynthia, whom I notice has streaks of blonde color in her hair. Two of Miss Anna Langer's daughters, Mina and Shanna are also there

The dream scene of the huge tree with very large roots, cut at the road, existed since my childhood. I took this dream as an insight into my eventual state of health. I would be able to get rid of the symbolic ants that were causing the weakness and pain in my body. The ants represented afflictions by the enemy.

This dream was a follow-up to the one I had in which I was chased by a cow and saw a tree, weakened by ants (Dream 3.10). I expect total healing of my body, as indicated by the success of me getting rid of all the ants, in this dream. In the end, I expect to be very strong as God showed by the symbolic big tree with very large roots.

(Dream 3.11, White Hand, 12/23/2006, Jenness)

I am at work. I am walking down the corridor with an empty bottle in my hand. The bottle looks like one that contains God's herb. I unscrew the cork. It falls out of my hand.

I am close to the bathroom, so I go inside to wash off the cork. While washing the cork I know someone else is using one of the toilets. Before I finish washing the cork, Betty, a white former coworker from Onela, comes out of the stall. As she is washing her hands, I am washing mine. I look at her hands and see they are white, which is her color. I look at my right hand and notice part of it is turning slightly white, but not as white as Betty's. I think to myself, "So this is what it means. That's not bad. Some people are bleaching themselves, anyway." I know my thinking refers to my previous dream in which my doctor told me she would combine January's and February's physicals.

This dream was yet another revelation from God as He guided me through the process of taking His herb, just as an earthly doctor would monitor his patient. In this dream, He was showing me I would have a slight reaction which was nothing to worry about.

A few days after the dream, I looked at my hand and saw a change in my skin tone. I then realized this was what the "white hand" in this dream was about. The day before my skin tone changed, I had drunk some Chinese herbal tea. It made me think it didn't interact well with God's herb. I was also taking the special calcium and magnesium vitamin at the same time; this was a mistake, due to two dreams from the enemy to counteract the works of God's herb. I stopped taking God's herb. Despite this, I saw good results from taking it. The feel of discomfort in my body was drastically reduced.

My skin tone returned to normal in less than a week. Once again God came true in His guidance with His herb. It was as if I had a physical doctor who was regulating my medicine.

(Dream 3.12, Add Grapefruit, 4/8/2007, Jenness)

I am in my kitchen looking out of a window that faces the highway. I know I am expecting somebody to come and tell me about God's herb. Soon I see a man and a woman walking along the highway on the side close to my house. I know they are coming to me. They are out of sight as they turn the corner. The lady appears in my living room. She is coming towards the kitchen. She is tall, slightly overweight, and in her late sixties. She does not say anything. She comes into the kitchen and goes directly to the kitchen counter opposite to the window I was looking through.

I see some yellow grapefruit on the kitchen counter. I see her with a knife. As she is about to cut the grapefruit, I quickly move towards her and grab the grapefruit away. I say to her, "You didn't even wash it." I take the grapefruit and knife away from her. I know she is doing this to add the grapefruit to the current formulation of God's herb. I usually wash fruits before cutting them. I go to the sink and wash the grapefruit. I pick up a strainer to strain the juice. The lady left without saying anything.

I was in the process of experimenting with the formula of God's herb. I tried three variations in the proportion of the ingredients. With my background in formulating and testing consumer products, I thought this was something I should try. With all three formulations, I had reduced the amount of grapefruit. In effect, I was formulating God's herb from scratch. I was doing it in faith, as indicated in a previous dream that told of a woman's sister making milk from scratch (Dream 4.2).

After seeing I was experimenting with the "unknown," my husband was discouraging me from taking God's herb, because he thought I didn't know what I was doing. I prayed to God to reveal to me if I should continue with His herb. I was taking it in faith, according to His promise of complete wellness (Dream 3.1).

The day after this dream, I looked in the kitchen where the lady was standing while attempting to cut the grapefruit. This was where we usually store food from the farmer's market. I was looking for some other food when I saw that yellow grapefruits were also there. I did not realize my husband had bought grapefruits. He had gone to the farmer's market the day before. However, he didn't always buy grapefruits.

In this dream God was showing me I shouldn't have used less grapefruit and I needed to add back the grapefruit I cut back on in the formula. I was overwhelmed with amazement as I saw how God was directing me so clearly. As indicated in the dream, I added the extra grapefruit to the formula before using it. I prayed to God and asked Him to tell His messenger I apologize for my behavior during her visit. In real life, I was the type of person who always washes food before using it, so I reacted the same way in the dream.

(Dream 3.13, Hide the Formula, 4/19/2007, Jenness)

I am in a building. I see a man writing on a blackboard. I know he is a judge. I want to talk to him to ask him about God's herb. There are a few people around, paying attention to what he is doing. I finally get the chance to go up to him. I ask him to tell me which of the variation in formulation of God's herb I should continue taking.

The judge goes to a computer and does a search. I see the result of his search. There are three formulas. I can see the first two elements making up the formulas.

I could not see all the formulas clearly. I ask him to print them out, so I can see it better. He prints them. When I go to the printer to pick up the printout, the printer is jammed. I remove a lot of the papers that were causing the jam. They are in pieces. Many of them look threaded.

After removing the papers, I go back to the judge and ask him to print the formulas again. He prints them. I go to pick up the printout. Just as I retrieve it I see a man coming towards us. I know I must hide the printout from him because he would want to know the formulas for God's herb. I find myself with a newspaper in my hand. I hide my printout in the newspaper. I start to walk away. I look on the ground and see an eyeglass. One lens is missing. I see the lens besides the eyeglass. The missing lens is broken in two. I realize this is my eyeglass. I think to myself, "It doesn't matter anyhow. I can see without them." I leave the eyeglass on the ground and keep walking.

I go outside. I realize I can see much better. I see a few people on the road. I realize my husband is behind me. I know I am ready to leave. He says to me, "What's the hurry." I decide to go without him.

I climb a small hill where I see a little girl. I know I am going to her house. I reach her house. My husband appears. He starts to look around in the kitchen for food. I say to him, "They just went shopping." He looks in the refrigerator and comes out with a rum bottle. He starts to drink directly from it. He puts back the little that is left.

God chose to reveal a part of His herb's formula to me (Dream 3.7). He did not want me to get discouraged. I believe with this dream I could discover the active ingredient in the formula of God's herb. God also indicated to me I should not reveal His formula to a man. The judge in the dream represents, God – The Father (John 8:50), as fitting to the interpretation by (Fishman 176).

God gave me further direction to encourage me and to promise more improvement in my eyesight. After I started taking God's herb, my vision improved slightly, I lost the blurriness from my vision (astigmatism); I am no longer sensitive to sunlight and lights from vehicles when I drive at nights. Before using God's herb, I had to used dark glasses during the day for the sunlight and while driving at nights to reduce the effects of the glare from the lights of the other vehicles.

On December 15, 2006, I visited my eye doctor. He had to lower the strength of my prescription, very slightly. When my eye doctor noticed the changes in my eyes during the exam, he asked me if I was taking any herb. I admitted to him I was taking an herb. However, I did not reveal anything further when he asked which herb. I only told him it was something I put together. The effect of God's herb on my eyesight was very pleasing to me, but not surprising, since I had noticed changes in my vision before I went to the eye doctor.

On April 14, 2007, my husband and I went to a friend's birthday party. It was a small crowd of people. After talking for a while with the other people, I learned one of the couples has a daughter who was doing research. I asked the lady to tell me more about the kind of research her daughter was doing because I was interested in research. After I said that, my husband jumped into the conversation and told everyone I was taking herb for my back problems. He mentioned the name of the main fruit after they asked about it. I had no intention of giving away the formulation like that. I was not happy that he was divulging information. Luckily, he only mentioned one of the ingredients. I remembered this dream while I was in the situation.

The alcohol my husband was drinking in the dream was related to the wine being served at the party.

(Dream 3.14, Films in Baby's Eyes, 12/05/2007, Jenness)

I am at a house. I know the house is mine. My family is gathered for the Christmas party my daughter, Sonia, planned. I see a little girl about two years old with her mother, Gina. I say to Gina, "Oh, so this is one of your children that I don't know." I look down and see one of the little girl's legs is slightly bent.

I walk further in the room. I see a dark baby lying on her back. I know she belong to my niece, Monica. The baby has a little snot in her nose. She opens her eyes and looks at me. I can see there are slight films in both her eyes and a few words written on top of the films, which have a few lines. I know she can see; but, will see better if the films are removed. I think to myself, "They need to wash her eyes with water."

On December 09, 2007, I started to feel something like debris in both eyes. I had to start washing my eyes with eyewash to get some relief. On December 13, 2007, I was sitting in the cafeteria at work when I took off my glasses and noticed slight improvement in my range of vision. Since I was still feeling debris in both eyes on and off, I decided to continue with eye washing once per day. I didn't have to continue this for too long before I washed away what my eyes were trying to get rid of.

As it turned out, there was a very slight improvement in my vision as well as cure from astigmatism of my eyes when I went to the eye doctor. I knew this was due to God's herb that I was taking for my back problems. This special herb was formulated, based on my sister, Catreen's, dream (Dream 3.7).

This dream was directing me ahead of time; I should wash my eyes with water before I was faced with the feeling of debris in my eyes. One again, Doctor God was instructing His patient on how to use His herb.

****

My recovery dream stories have taken you through the many formats of how God gives guidance, gift, and revelations through dreams. His promise of complete wellness, in a dream, is one I hang onto with unflinching faith; so much so that I wrote God a note to, *"Heal my flesh and reset my bones,"* dated and signed it.

It is obvious to me, that as I overcome more of my spiritual battles it brings healing to my body and my face changes to be younger looking. I do not have to wonder how I got over the many challenges I faced along the way. I know God was the Mighty Ocean that washed over my soul and set my spirit free from oppression and suppression.

The special cure of God's herb for my back problem was immunization against spiritual afflictions. His guidance through the process of formulating and taking His herb was one that brought me to a higher spiritual level of total surrender as I put all my trust in God. In all this, I gained a much deeper understanding of my God. As He heals my body and spirit, my soul and mind are uplifted.

Chapter 4

Called to Be a Spiritual Warrior

My calling is to be a spiritual warrior and God showed me this in many different types of dreams. He initially showed this calling in dreams, but it continues into reality. God has unique ways of calling individuals. It is for you to pay attention to the signs God is showing you.

Pay attention to unusual changes in your life. The dream stories in this chapter tell of ways God used to show me my spiritual calling. He indicated that He would multiply my money and use me to cause people to go to church in droves. Later, God anointed me as a spiritual warrior to destroy Satan's kingdom on earth. This calling on my life took me through rigorous on-the-battle-field training. I went to Hell and back. However, Jesus was with me all the time – doing the training. I humbly wear God's warrior badge on my heart. I feel honored to be selected for God's mission.

(Dream 4.1, Praise You Lord Forever, 11/17/2005, Jenness)

I am watching a man filming a gospel video. Men and women are dancing as they sing a song. I am enjoying the singing as I watch.

After the song finishes, I see the famous American singer, Mariah Carey, and a lady practicing to sing a very beautiful song of praise. It is a song I never heard before. The lady keeps faltering on one of the verses while Mariah can handle it. After a while, the lady turns out to be me. The song gives me a joyful feeling. After the third trial, Mariah decides to leave. She is disgusted that I keep faltering while singing.

After Mariah leaves, I find myself singing a song I am familiar with – "I want to thank you Lord with all that is within me. I want to sing the song that you have given me. I want to praise you Lord forever, forever and forever. Lord You have been so good to me."

I woke up singing the song in my mind over and over and over. This dream was a revelation. At the time, I had been totally engrossed in religious music after I had the dream in which I was feeling completely well in my body (Dream 3.1). This dream inspires me to write my own song of praise to God after my healing is complete. I believe the song to be written is the glorious song in the dream, of which, I cannot recall one word. At the time of this dream, I was listening to some great gospel music, but the song I heard in the dream was beyond anything I have ever heard.

I have come to realize God loves songs. He has been directing me not only in dreams but also through spiritual incidents, some of which involve songs. God used selected songs to help me fight spiritual battles and to praise and worship Him. While going through my spiritual battles, God allowed me to promise Him to write songs for Him. I know that when I eventually write these songs they will be very pleasing to God and will be of a quality that has not been heard before. The dream indicated it would have to be song by Mariah Carey or someone of her caliber.

As a spiritual warrior, I come to realize songs are also weapons to be used in overcoming Satan. After all, Satan was an angel in Heaven, so even he knows the power of songs. He not only had the covering of every precious stone – sardius, topaz, diamond, beryl, onyx, jasper, sapphire, emerald, carbuncle, and gold, but also was created with musical instruments – tabrets and pipes (Ezekiel 28:13). Therefore, he would want to lay claim to the music industry. We can arm ourselves with the right songs when fighting against the works of Satan.

(Dream 4.2, Homemade Milk, 2/8/2006, Jenness)

My younger daughter, Sonia, my sister, Ruth, and I are sitting at a table having dinner with a white Jewish family. The odd thing is that only the husband sits at the table with us. The wife and her sister are sitting in an enclosure near the dining table, eating their dinner. As I sit, I am thinking, "Maybe the wife cannot sit at the table with her husband because of Jewish tradition. Yet, the husband sits to eat with us because we are different."

The husband's features are quite distinct, and I can see his face clearly. He is medium built in stature, about six feet tall, and handsome. The husband finishes his meal and leaves us at the table to go into the kitchen. After that, his wife's sister joins us at the table.

I decide to have some milk to drink. It is in a traditional Jamaican "Tastee Cheese" container. I am shocked it tastes so very good. I say to the wife's sister, "I never tasted milk so good before." She replies, "She made it from scratch." I know she is referring to her sister. I drink most of the milk and leave a little in the container.

I get up from the table and go into the kitchen. The husband is still in the kitchen. I see a lot of food – fried fish, vegetables, and rice. I go back to the dining room and sit down. I reach for the container I left with milk and see it is almost empty. The wife's sister says to me, "I drank the rest of it." She reaches for the container and passes it to me. There is very little left in the container, so I pour it out and drink it.

The milk is symbolic of God nourishing me spiritually. It serves to strengthen me as a warrior of God. He had shown me He would be providing me with special milk, made from scratch – feeding me with the milk of His word, as a newborn baby, and directing my spiritual growth (I Peter 2:2). Also, according to Fishman, milk represents "The elementary teachings of the Christian faith (Hebrew 5:12), (142). I know that elementary Christian teachings for my sister, Ruth, and me have been taking place through Jesus Christ of Nazareth, Himself.

The next morning after I had this dream I told my sister, Ruth, about it. She said milk traditionally means spiritual bread and the family we dined with being Jewish, only confirmed it had to do with our spiritual wellbeing. It turned out Ruth was correct in her interpretation. During my many encounters with spiritual wickedness, God conducted warfare training of Ruth and me from "*scratch.*" I did not even have time to read anything about spiritual warfare before my real battlefield training started.

(Dream 4.3, It Is Found in Romans, 10/10/2006, Jenness)

There are some people walking around in my house, checking it out. I know they are looking to buy it. I pull the curtains apart to let in more light. It becomes very bright, so I pull the curtains together.

I move to another room. I notice a young girl and a child. The phone rings. The young girl says, "It is for Dassa. I never heard of that name before." I think to myself, "It is from the Bible."

My mother then appears. Her name is Adassa, but some people called her Dassa. I tell her to answer the phone. She doesn't. Instead she hands me a small New Testament Bible and says, "It is in Romans." I start flipping through the Bible, but I'm not sure of what I am looking for.

I tell my mother again to answer the phone. She is just standing in front of me watching while I flip through the Bible, looking for what I am not sure of. It seems as if she has no intention of answering the phone.

The next morning, I wondered if what I dreamt meant my late mother was telling me that God was calling me to be with her as an apostle, on the other side. Or, was I called to be an apostle of God while on earth? I say this because, God had indicated to me, in a dream, that she was with His saints, before He started using her in dreams to the family. I looked for my New Testament Bible but couldn't find it. I did not have any other Bible in the house.

I remembered that a co-worker, Wayne, always had a New Testament Bible on his desk at work. As soon as I arrived at work, I borrowed the Bible from his desk. I opened the Bible to where I believed I should find the book of Romans. As God would have it, the first page I opened the Bible to was Romans chapter one. I was deeply moved by what I read.

Opening the Bible to exactly Romans chapter one to read its content was God's way of notifying me I am called to be His apostle on earth. He used the example of Paul, who being a servant of Jesus Christ was called to be an apostle and separated to preach the gospel of God. I decided to search through the entire book of Romans in the Holy Bible, looking for verses that had to do with call. I found Romans

1:1-13; 2:17; 8:28-30; 9:7; 9:24-26; and 10:12-13 to be relevant to the calling of God on my life. Like, Paul, I am called to be an apostle of God and separated to do His work. My apostleship calling was appointed by Jesus Christ as He appeared to me in a dream when I was about four years old.

I came to realize my apostleship will have worldwide reach, according to the direction in which God is currently leading me. It will take me into serving my God with my spirit as God has been imparting spiritual gifts to me to be used in His company. God's company, Works Of Trinity, LLC, is a unique way in which God is using commerce to draw people closer to Him. It will have multinational outreach so that others can learn of their Creator and bear fruits of the spirit of God.

It is at this point in life that my purpose on earth has been identified. With the love of God in my heart, my apostleship will be doing good works unto Him. I was predestinated to conform to the image of Jesus Christ. Therefore, I am called, justified, and glorified (Romans 8:29-30). God called not only the Jews, but also the Gentiles. I have been identified as a child of God. He makes no difference between the Jews and others; for God is Lord over all of us. We just must call on His name and believe in Jesus Christ to be saved.

(Dream 4.4, Money Multiplied in Church, 12/15/2006, Jenness)

I am in a car with my daughter, Sonia. It is parked outside of a church. I notice a car with a Jewish family pulls up. They are going to the same church. I enter the church and the Jewish family follows. I can see the features of the father distinctly but not of the rest of his family. He sits in the pulpit area, but not with his family. I sit with the regular congregation. The church is about forty five percent full.

After a while I see my daughter, Kristal, to the right of me. She is walking out the door with a lighted cigarette in her hand. I become concerned and decide to follow her out.

Outside, I see her smoking with a young black man. I slap the cigarette out of Kristal's hand and slap her on her face. She is upset with me. I decide to go back into the church.

When I return they are in the process of collecting offering. I see my money purse on the bench and open it. I have some coins in it and a few dollars. As I am feeling for the coins to pull some out for the offering, the dollars multiplied into much more. They are all crumpled up, so I cannot see the amount on the bill. I decide instead of coins I will give some of the bills as offering.

On March 28, 2010, I saw the fulfillment of this dream. I went to church on Palm Sunday. As I went in, I saw a table spread with some food, flowers, and two candles on it. I never had communion at that church before, so I assumed it had something to do with the way they did their communion.

During the part of the service where we greet each other with a hug or handshake, I greeted a woman who had the strong smell of cigarette on her breath. After that, there was the call for the offering. I did not bring much money with me because I had already written a check and brought it with me. When the bishop requested that the congregation put a little extra offering, since it was Passover, I looked in my change purse and saw I had six crumpled dollar bills. I then recalled this dream with the cigarette incident, followed by offering, and then followed by crumpled dollar bills. I felt that God wanted me to pay special attention to the preaching, which would take place later.

A white, woman, Dr. Collins, was introduced earlier as a visitor, but I did not know she would be preaching. When she was introduced as the preacher and we were told she would be doing the Jewish Passover with us, the other part of the dream with the Jewish family in church with me was fulfilled. However, instead of a man sitting at the pulpit area, it was a Jewish woman.

I learned Jesus fulfilled Jewish traditions as the sacrificial lamb without spot, as they would use in the Old Testament days. One other thing that stood out was the many major Biblical events that happened around Passover, such as the children of Israel marking their doors with the blood of lamb. This gave me the clue to look out for God to multiply my money around Passover time, as a major event in my life.

Another thing that stood out in Dr. Collins' preaching was the act of Jesus folding the cloth that was tied around His head after He rose from the dead. She explained it as an act of insult if someone folded the napkin after being invited to dinner at a Jewish home. It indicated the person was displeased and would never return. It was how the disciples who visited the tomb knew Jesus had risen.

This was not the first dream I had about Jewish family. Seeing this one fulfilled is confirmation that as a soldier in the army of God, one of my missions will be to convince the Jews that they have mistakenly rejected Jesus Christ as their Messiah. I know I have been called by Jesus

Christ to be an apostle for Him and as such, am willing to take on this task.

(Dream 4.5, People Come to Church for Drugs, 12/15/2006, Jenness)

I am in a car with two white men. I know I am getting a ride to somewhere. The driver says he has to stop and drop off something and we wouldn't have to get out of the car. After a while, he stops at a building. The driver gets out of the car with a package.

I start to get the feeling that the place belongs to the Mafia. A man comes out of the building and orders the other man and me out of the car. We come out and go into the building. I realize this building is a church. There is a small amount of people inside, waiting for the service to start.

I go to the window and stand, looking out. The driver of the car comes and stands with me. I see many people driving up, coming to the church. They are all white; except for one beautiful, fair skinned, black, lady who comes right up to the window, stares me in the face for a while, then goes away. I start thinking, "People are coming to church to buy drugs. They are using the church as a cover for trafficking drugs." I am thinking of the herb I was taking which I refer to as God's herb.

On October 4, 2006, I met a Spanish woman on the train that resembled the one in this dream. She asked me if I knew anyone who had "*O negative*" blood. She was very distraught. She explained to me that her son was dying from leukemia and needed blood. I told her to give me her contact information because I have a sister who was "*O negative.*"

God allowed me to meet this woman with the sick son so that when He is ready to heal the son, I would be able to contact his mother.

God chose to show me what the result of my work for Him would be in the future. People would be coming to church in large numbers for healing.

(Dream 4.6, Blacks Coming to Church, 1/5/2007, Jenness)

I am in a church. I know the church is in the community where I grew up. The church is empty except for me and another woman.

I go to the door to greet people. A lot of people start to come in. Some of them are people I grew up with. One of them, Dit, is at the door with me. The church becomes packed with people and I can see more coming.

God was showing me once again that as His anointed warrior, I would be playing a key role in bringing people to church. After having the dream about white people coming to church in droves for drugs (Dream 4.5), I started wondering if God's herb would only benefit them. God allowed me to have this dream to show me His herb was for everyone.

(Dream 4.7, God's Mission, 2/21/2007, Jenness)

I am in a church. My sisters, Petra and Ruth, are also there. We are singing a hymn while communion is being served. I know this church has changed somewhat. I see that the bread is being passed around in a small plastic cup. I think to myself, "It is because they are joined to another type of church."

As the cup gets passed around people take out a piece of the bread. The cup is passed to me. I see that the bread is a small piece of zucchini with the inside looking dark brown. I take a piece of the zucchini.

I find myself sitting down in front of my husband. He is sitting along the roadway; cutting away on a piece of zucchini-like material with a knife. The inside is also dark brown.

I feel overwhelmed with honor. I start to cry as I tell my husband, "God is ready for me to leave on His mission." It is as if he doesn't see or hear me. He is totally focused on cutting away on the zucchini-like material. I can literally feel the emotion of overwhelming honor because of the realization that God is ready for me to go on His mission. I am crying tears of honor and humiliation. I cry for a while.

God was showing me it was getting closer to the time for me to go on His mission.

On April 2, 2007, my neighbor invited me to her church for a special remembrance of the death of Jesus. I decided I would go with her.

She was a Jehovah Witness. They had readings from various parts of the Bible, after which they passed around unleavened bread. It was strange to me that they simply passed around the bread from person to person without breaking and eating it. That was followed by the wine, which they again passed around without drinking. This reminded me of the dream. I thought of it as an indication of God's mission for me getting close to the time.

As it turned out, God's mission was revealed in 2008 as part of my training in handling spiritual attacks. I felt as if I were in spiritual boot camp, based on the many forms of spiritual attacks I had to deal with. To be a spiritual warrior, it is necessary that you get the proper training. My experiences are written about in the book, *God's Mission: Spiritual Battles and Revelation of Anti-666*.

(Dream 4.8, Train to Be a Leader, 4/12/2007, Jenness)

I am at a place. There are some people around. I get the feeling I am at work. I see two women working. I know they are in training. A man says to me, "They are training for women's leadership. Why don't you do that?" I say to him, "I don't know. I am not sure."

The company I am working with has a training program to retain women in leadership positions. I know that is what the man is talking about.

This dream has been fulfilled in the reality of me going through brutal spiritual battles as part of my training to help those who are going through the same experience. During my experience, I promised God to help others who were going through similar experiences. As such, I will be taking on a lead role in helping people overcome spiritual wickedness.

More recently, the reality of my leadership became more vivid. I was directed by God to form His company for saving souls. God's company is of a commercial nature and not the traditional ministries, church, or religious organization.

(Dream 4.9, Do I Look Like an Angel, 5/11/2007, Jenness)

I am outside a building with a lot of people. I see my friend, Donna, some distance away. She has on a very white lacy crown that is supposed to be a nurse's cap. She touches it and I hear her says to a young girl, "Do I look like an angel?"

Donna then walks over to me and says, "I have a present for you." She gives me a box. I decide not to wait to open it. I open the box and take out a very white lacy bra, just as white as the crown I saw Donna with. I decide to fit it over my breast.

This dream indicated the relative spiritual ranking of Donna and me. Later, I found out, while going through some spiritual attacks she was at a higher spiritual level than I was. As I indicated in this dream with the white pieces of clothing, the head is higher than the breast. However, I find my level of spirituality to be constantly increasing as I fight and overcome spiritual battles.

The ultimate reward is to be crowned as an angel after God calls us home.

(Dream 4.10, See Far Without Glasses, 5/15/2007, Jenness)

I am in a building. I am standing at a counter. The guy behind the counter hands me my eyeglasses. I put them on.

I look at a board in the far distance. I can see the writings clearly. I take off my glasses and put them in the case. Again, I look at the board in the far distance. I can see the writings just as clearly without my glasses. I am surprised I can see that clearly. It is as if I am seeing in real life.

God was showing me that one day I would be able to see things in the supernatural realm as clearly as in the natural realm.

****

The dreams in this chapter are just the stories of my early spiritual journey. My spiritual calling took me through some very rough paths; so rough that I felt like a soldier in the forefront of war against spiritual evil in this world. These experiences are written about in two of my books: *God's Mission: Spiritual Battles and Revelation of Anti-666* and *God Has Gone Corporate*.

In the beginning of my journey with God, He showed me that He is calling me to be a spiritual warrior and an apostle for Him. Next, He showed me He would nourish me spiritually, as with spiritual milk. God allowed me to use songs in fighting my battles. He showed me that I would be helping others and because of my work, they would be going to churches in record numbers. Finally, God gave me a glimpse of my future where there would be no barrier to my spirituality. I would see things clearly in the supernatural.

Chapter 5
Dreams of Death

Dreams that predict death are sometimes fulfilled while others are just warnings of death. Dreamers can sometimes prevent danger if they pay attention to these dreams. This chapter is dedicated to the dream stories surrounding the deaths of my mother and sister. For both, the family was forewarned of their upcoming deaths. However, we did not pray against their deaths; we just accepted them aforehand. The dreams for each of them tell a story of its own.

I know some believers might object to dreams in which God is using the dead. (Isaiah 8:19) warns us not to seek after those with familiar spirits and those who work magic; seek after God and not after the dead. You are advised to join to all that are living, as a living dog is better than a dead lion; the dead does not know anything and has no say on anything that is done on earth (Ecclesiastic 9:4-6). Neither my sister, Ruth, nor I sought to communicate with our deceased relatives; some people do so by devilish means. God first warned us that they were going to died, then after their deaths, He indicated to us that they are with His saints; next, He started using them in the initial stages of our battles with evil spirits; after we were at a stage of our journey where we recognized what we were facing and dealing with it, He stopped using them.

I prayed a lot regarding writing about the role of my deceased relatives in my spiritual journey. Jesus Christ of Nazareth is always faithful. He allowed me to reflect on all that I went through and all that I accomplished for Him. I am writing about my experiences because He asked it of me. In response to my prayers, He lead me to scriptures where He addressed matters of the dead and living. In a parable about the rich man and Lazarus, Jesus indicated that those who died in Him are at a place of comfort, while others are at a place of torment – Hell; people on either sides can see each other, but cannot cross the great gulf (divide) between them; according to the argument between Abraham and the rich man in Hell, Lazarus could have gone back to warn the rich man's brothers so that they could repent; however, Abraham pointed out that they have the living – Moses and other prophets to whom they should listen (Luke 16:19-31).

In the book of John, Jesus spoke of the Father raising the dead and giving them life, and He also can do the same to whom He pleases. He spoke of the day when the dead will hear His voice. (John 5:21). Even after reflecting on many scriptures about the dead, I realize the power of God in my situation to accomplish His end-time works. At this point, you will not fully grasp why I say this; you must read more about my stories to understand.

God allowed my sister and me to first have dreams that indicated the spirits of my mother and sister went to Heaven, before He started using them in many important dreams He gave us. I personally do not place a limit on God. He is eternal – existed before time, within time, and beyond time; He is in command of everything known to mankind and unknown to mankind. I know God can use anything He so desires to get His message across, especially when it is something or someone who will grab the attention of the intended person.

My Mother

Although my mother did not share her dreams with me, my niece, Rose, told me that my mother was a spiritual dreamer. We called our mother, Ansa. Her first child attempted to mimic calling her Aunt Dassa. However, at her age, she could only formulate the pronunciation "*Ansa.*" All the other siblings adopted that nickname for our mom.

Ansa was a God-fearing woman who raised her twelve children, seven girls and five boys, in the neighboring Presbyterian Church. She is now deceased.

Before Ansa died, God gave me indications of her death, through dreams. After her death, I was given the reassurance that she was with the God's saints. God used her to communicate with us through dreams after she died. She forewarned us about things that would be happening to us. It seemed that God later passed on most of my mother's responsibility to my sister, Catreen, once she too went to be with Him.

(Dream 5.1, Auntlyn And Carl Won't Make It in Time, 9/9/2004, Jenness)

I am one of many people taking shelter from the hurricane in a building with wide open space. Elsa, my deceased sister, comes to me and gives me a sheet of paper. She says to me, "Ansa said to write that Auntlyn and Carl wouldn't make it in time." I complain, "What's the use of doing this when Auntlyn is dead," Elsa says, "I want you to give it to Ansa,"

I still hesitate. She insists, so I take the piece of paper and write on it. I give back the sheet of paper to her. She draws two clocks on it with the time and writes some words. I cannot see the words clearly. I am unable to figure out the time. She then gives me the paper.

After Elsa leaves, I see a few of my nieces and nephews from my deceased brother, Collin. They are also in the same building, seeking shelter from the hurricane. I can literally hear the rain pounding on the roof.

I woke up to heavy rain pounding on the roof that night, during the hurricane season of 2004. Jamaica was in the direct path of Hurricane Ivan. My other sisters and I were concerned about our country and family over there. I was praying to God for their protection. Ivan was a rare category five hurricane, with winds up to 165 miles per hour. My interpretation of the dream was that my mother and brother, Carl, would die in the hurricane.

Jamaica is a nation of God-fearing people with most of the population believing in God. The entire country was praying to God to spare them from the hurricane. The power of prayer was proven when Ivan, originally headed for

Jamaica changed direction at the last minute, leaving torrential rains in its path instead.

The two clocks in the dream represented two deaths in my family. I suspected who it would be but didn't know the times.

As suggested in the dream, I wrote a letter that told my mother about it and warned her to prepare her soul to go to Heaven because my dream indicated she would die. My mother died one year after I had this dream. The other clock belonged to my sister, Catreen. She died eight months after my mom. In the dream I could not tell the time on the clocks; that's probably why the deaths, less than two years later were unexpected for both.

(Dream 5.2, Radio Announcement – Woman Found Dead, 1/31/2006, Jenness)

I am at my mother's house, in her room, listening to the news on the radio. The announcer reads, "The body of an unidentified woman is found." I then find myself with a piece of paper with only the signature SN written on it. I realize this is what they found on the woman.

Soon after, I have another piece of paper in my hands. It has the woman's name and address. I can see the name clearly but not the address. The name clearly is "Annie Henry." I am shocked to find it is my cousin. We call her Tina.

    I leave the room to go to the adjoining one and look out the window. It is as if I know I will find people under the window. I see my deceased Uncle Jossy; deceased Aunt, Jean, the mother of Tina; and a few other old people I do not recognize. I know the others are also relatives who were passed on. They are all engaged in conversation. I call out to my Uncle Jossy and tell him, "Tina is found dead."

    I go looking for my sister Ruth to tell her the news. I find Ruth in the nearby churchyard arguing with a boy. My daughter, Sonia, and niece Berta are playing with a group of children in the area and apparently the boy is the captain. From what I gather, Ruth is protesting something about the game, relating to Sonia. I go up to the boy and say, "I am the mother."

    I then turn my attention to Ruth and say to her, "We have to leave and find Petra because Tina is found dead and we have to go." I feel sadness and at the same time a sense of urgency. We leave the children playing and warn them to behave while we are gone. We decide we also must find our cousin, Liza, and tell her the news.

This dream was the second forewarning of my mother's death. Being warned ahead of time made it a little easier to take, even though the suddenness of the news was painful.

The deceased lady in the dream identified as Tina turned out to be my mother. My mother's death was announced twice on the radio, as part of the funeral home's package.

I was staying at my sister, Ruth's house when around 4:00 a.m. on February 26, 2006, the phone rang. We knew right away it couldn't be for a good reason, considering the time of the night. It was my other sister, Petra, on the phone. She said she got a call from our cousin, Betty, who told her our nephew, Joey, called to tell her our mother might be dead. Betty was going to investigate and then call back. We were shocked to hear of our mother's death since she was only suffering from mild diabetes and high blood pressure. We got a follow-up call from Petra that confirmed our mother had passed on.

(Dream 5.3, She Is with The Saints by The River, 2/28/2006, Jenness)

I find myself in the church I used to attend while growing up. My mother's body is lying in her coffin. I go up to the coffin and see that her face is covered. I remove the cover from her face. I am fascinated to see she looks so young. I keep staring at her face for a while; thinking, "She looks so good. There is not even a wrinkle in her face."

I decide to touch my mother on her foot. In response to that, her body moves slightly to the right, towards me, with her eyes still closed.

My sister, Petra, is in the church. I call to her and say, "Let us sing, we will gather at the river, the beautiful, beautiful river, gather with the saints by the river that flows from the throne of God."

I woke up from my sleep crying. I knew the dream meant my mother's spirit ascended to Heaven; she had made it safely home. God showed me that my mother made it to be with His saints. My mother died on the night of February 25, 2006; early morning of the 26th. I had this dream on the night of February 28, 2006, the third day after her death, which was when her spirit would be expected to ascend to Heaven.

The song's lyric in the dream about gathering with the saints by the river is a testimony to my mother being with the Lord. I kept crying for about half an hour. I did not cry when I got the news that my mother died because I was prepared for that, based on a previous dream I had about the two clocks (Dream 5.1). I cried for joy to know she made it safely to be with God's saints.

I told this dream at her funeral service because I knew my mother would want others to know she had made it to Heaven.

(Dream 5.4, She Is on The Other Side, 10/11/2006, Jenness)

I am somewhere outside a building. I am not sure where I am. I see my mother. I know she comes to visit me. I ask her, "How are you doing?" She says, "I am bored." I ask her, "Have you seen Auntlyn?" She replies, "Yes. But, she is on the other side. She is working to come over."

God revealed to me my aunt, Auntlyn, did not make it to the same place as my mother. She is my mother's deceased sister and my favorite aunt. However, she is doing work to try and make it to the same side my mother is on. This dream serves as a lesson. My aunt was a Christian and very active in her church. I thought at first, she did not make it to Heaven. However, God is faithful in helping me to understand this dream.

Dreams of Death

On February 23, 2012, my sister called me at work. At some point in the conversation she told me she would really like to understand the dream I had about Auntlyn not been on the same side as Ansa. I told her I would also like to understand it myself.

Later at home, I felt determined to read some of the experiences of Heaven and Hell that people wrote about at www.spiritlessons.com. After I read a few, I came upon the experience of Reverend Park. Based on his experience of Heaven, I was able to understand this dream. As two angels showed Reverend Park around, he saw that not everyone was at the same place and not everyone had the same kind of house built for them. Some had huge mansions, some had homes looking like fowl coop, and some had no homes. The angels explained some people barely made it to Heaven on salvation and didn't have homes built because they were not doing anything on earth to be rewarded in Heaven, or what they were doing were not from the heart. God rewards us according to what He sees in our hearts (Reverend Park, Yong Gyu). With that being said, it is better to barely make it to Heaven than to be in Hell.

My Sister, Catreen

My older sister, Catreen, had been through many trials and tribulations while on this earth. Very shortly after she went to the other side, God used her as a very powerful angel who He quickly sent to guide me through my spiritual battles. It seemed as if she quickly took over from our mother in providing Ruth and I with spiritual guidance. I know it was God Who was using her so that we would pay special attention to the dreams He was giving us.

The level of care and guidance God provided through Catreen during the early stages of my battles with evil spirits, caused both Ruth and I to appreciate her more than when she was alive. Her strength and determination really came through for us. Catreen's dream story consists of dreams from more than one persons.

(Dream 5.5, Carrying Catreen's Casket, 02/12/2005, Jenness)

I am at the community where I grew up. I am with a crowd of people following a casket. They are carrying the casket towards my mother's house. I know it is my sister, Catreen, who they are carrying to be buried. I think to myself, "She died because James is giving her a lot of problems."

This dream was fulfilled. Catreen died a year later; although not because of problems with her son, James. At first, I was interpreting the dream that it was meant for my other sister, Ruth, since she was caring for James and at times there would be conflicts.

I called Ruth and told her about the dream. She acknowledged that she was stressed out from dealing with James. It was only after Catreen died that I realized this was a direct dream and I had applied it to Ruth, incorrectly.

(Dream 5.6, My Spirit Will Ascend, 7/23/2006, Ruth)

I am lying on a long object and it is as if my spirit is looking at my body. I am being dressed and I am telling someone that is taking care of the body to prop up my head part a little more. I can feel my body move. I tell the people around that tomorrow my spirit will ascend to God.

This dream is a contribution from my sister, Ruth. It was fulfilled in a relative way. Instead of Ruth dying with a situation of her head being propped up, it was Catreen. The dream was indicating Catreen would go to Heaven when she died. She died at Ruth's house. Ruth had to call the ambulance when she found her slumped down in the bathroom. When the paramedics were taking care of Catreen's body they asked for a towel to prop up her head.

Long after Catreen's body was transferred from the hospital to the funeral parlor, Ruth went to view her body. She saw how much Catreen's countenance changed. Her face was bright and glowing. She looked so good and peaceful. At that point, the reality of this dream hit Ruth. She realized Catreen's spirit ascended to Heaven and caused such a change in her body. Shortly after this dream, Ruth had another dream in which Catreen was telling her she made it to the *"right side,"* meaning Heaven. She told Ruth, *"I was serving God, but you did not believe me."*

(Dream 5.7, Mother Is Watching Me, 09/24/2006, Jenness)

I am walking down a road with a few people. The road steeps downward. I look to my right and see my mother watching me. I am happy to see her. I go over to her and hug her. She says to me, "Tell Ruth not to worry about Catreen."

Catreen died one month after this dream. Ruth would not have to worry about her anymore. At the time of this dream, my sister, Ruth, usually dealt with a lot of problems whenever Catreen got sick. She told me one day it was too much, and she had spoken out loudly that she needs help with Catreen. My mother was sending a message to let her know it would be over soon.

(Dream 5.8, Taking Catreen to the Doctor, 10/29/2006, Jenness)

I am with a crowd of people who are taking my sister, Catreen, to the doctor. As I am walking along, I notice a black, medium built man in his late fifties to early sixties, walking along, suspiciously. I know he is watching to see what will happen to Catreen.

The crowd of people gathers around Catreen and I cannot see her. I stand a little away from the crowd, so I can keep a constant watch on the suspicious looking man. Finally, the man approaches me and says, "Do you have mortgage?" I get very upset at him and replies in an angry tone, "She is my sister."

This dream occurred at the time when Catreen was in the process of dying and at the time of the dream, my husband and I were in the process of refinancing our mortgage.

I woke up to the ringing of the phone at about 5:40 a.m. It was my daughter, Kristal; while crying she said,

"Aunt Ruth called and said Aunt Catreen might be dead. She found her in the bathroom, stumped over. She called 911 and the ambulance is at her house." I hung up the phone and called Ruth's house. Her tenant, Sandy, answered and said the emergency service was working on Catreen and she was breathing a little. They were going to take her to the hospital. I felt better to hear she was breathing a little.

I went to work. I once again called Ruth's house and was told Catreen was dead. I was shocked because I was with her the evening before. She had planned on visiting the doctor about a bad cold, the day she died. I had plane tickets for both of us to go to Jamaica in two weeks. I was shocked, disappointed, and grieved. We had such great plans together. We were supposed to go home and investigate the herb she dreamt about. I felt she left me alone to handle it and I was faced with the burden of doing it for both of us.

(Dream 5.9, Baby Out of Breath, 11/3/2006, Jenness)

I am in a house. I see a form like my sister, Catreen. She is somewhat faded. She comes to me with a baby wrapped in a blanket. She says to me, "Help the baby."

When I look at the baby I can see she is gasping for breath.

I pull out my right breast and try to squeeze milk into a cup. A drop of milk comes out. After that only water comes out no matter how much I squeeze. I feel desperate and feel that time is against me. I finally reach out to get the baby.

I had this dream less than a week after Catreen died. She was showing me how she died, because she died of breathing problem. The desperation I felt and the realization I had of running out of time was how Catreen felt when she was dying. This was the first time God used Catreen to allow me to feel sensations in dreams which helped me to interpret situations. I had two other dreams in which God used her to allow me to feel the strong and mighty power of God and the hazy, sun-dazed feeling of extreme exhaustion, which can drive you crazy.

This death dream story about my sister, Catreen caused me to reflect on her. I had misinterpreted my dream about her coffin being carried to be warning about my other sister, Ruth. I was very impressed when God used Catreen to give me a dream in which she demonstrated how she died and allowed me to feel the anxiety she had when dying.

God knew that I would be very grieved by her passing and allowed her to leave me with some songs; one of which has the words, *"Not my will, but Thine be done great Jesus."* Just hearing those words allowed me to accept her passing as the will of God. I later realized her passing was part of the mission God had for me, using her to help me from *"the other side."*

Although some of these dream stories reflected unheeded death warnings for Catreen, at some point she had taken them seriously and was prepared to be with God. I remembered her telling me she believed she was going to die because she was having a lot of dreams about our deceased mother in which she was cooking for her and taking care of her.

****

These dream stories show other ways of looking at dreams about death. Your traditional means of interpretation, or those you might look up in dream book, might not be relevant to the situation.

We should always be prepared for death. If you have death dreams about people you should share it with them so that they can prepare themselves for a Heavenly home. You can also pray about the death dream, so that God can prevent the death of the person, if He so desires. I know I was successful in allowing my mother to prepare for her death. Luckily, Catreen was having her own death-related dreams that allowed her to prepare herself. I was not interpreting her death dreams correctly. Since she was not that old, I was not willing to accept the possibility of death for her.

Chapter 6

Warnings of My Possible Death

This chapter has a collection of dreams that point to my possible death, in one form or the other. These dreams are not all mine; other family members were having dreams that indicated death was on the horizon for me.

(Dream 6.1, Resting in Peace, 3/12/2003, Jenness)

I am at the dormitory where I used to board while going to high school. One particularly large room has many bunk beds. I am in this room, lying on one of the top bunk beds. I physically feel rested and quite at peace.

After a while, I see a few black women walking up toward me as if curious as to who I am. I realize they are all ghosts. I feel a little scared and start to repeat the 23rd Psalm – "The Lord is my shepherd I shall not want ..." When they come close enough, I realize they are friendly. I stop saying the Psalm.

After abruptly ending repetition of the 23rd Psalm, I notice a young girl on another bunk bed, close to mine. She says to me, "I think you will pup (pass gas) in a crowd." I reply, "Yes."

My bed is close to a window. I notice two black men outside the window looking at me. It is as if they, too, are curious about me being there. One of them wears dreadlocks. He says to me, "I can find your father for you." I reply, "Do you know my father?" Both men go away after I respond.

This dream indicated it is well with my soul because of the sense of peace and rest I had while among the dead. It gave me reassurance of the destiny of my soul. I was close to two years old when my father died. I have no memory of him whatsoever. I am sure I would not be able to identify him if I should see him in the *"afterlife."* Someone would have to point him out to me. Being at a place where I had good memories and feeling such sense of rest and peace among dead people was telling me something positive about my *"afterlife."*

I interpreted the dream as my soul finding rest when I die. God gave me that reassurance. I took comfort in knowing where my soul would end up when I die. I got a happy feeling about it. I didn't let what was going on around me bother me too much; after all, it is well with my soul. While doing my final edit and reading the comments for this dream, God reminded me of the battle I had to evict the 666 demon out of the church I was attending a few years ago. During this battle, Psalm 23:1-4 was relevant; the Lord was shepherding me as I faced possible death from evil spirits, but I was not afraid, since I knew He was with me; and as a weapon in this battle, He gave me the song, *"It is well with my soul."*

(Dream 6.2, Perfume, 4/21/2007, Jenness)

I put a key in a door and open it. I realize I am inside the church I used to attend while growing up. The side towards the door I entered from has light, but the other parts are in semi-darkness. The church is empty. I look towards my right and see two blankets covering up something. I wonder, "Is there a body under the sheets?"

Suddenly, I am in a place with my sister, Ruth. The area where we stand has light, but the other side is in semi-darkness. A door to my right opens. I see my mother comes through it. She looks happy, but she is walking with a very long stick. I notice she is not limping, as if there is any need to be walking with a stick. The stick is rough looking like the ones you would put to support plants. It is much taller than her.

I am happy to see my mother. I run to her and hug her. She says, "Catreen and I want Siji Diamond perfume." I say, "I will get it." Ruth gets upset and says, "No, I will get it." She leaves and goes into the dark area. While Ruth is gone, I notice some clothes hanging in a closet. I start to take out one at a time and look at it. I want to see which one is suitable to wear. I say to my mother, "Is Catreen going also?" She says, "Yes." I know they are planning to go somewhere.

Ruth comes back with a perfume and gives it to me. I take a little from it and touch it on my mother's stomach. I can literally smell the perfume. I give the perfume to my mother and she leaves.

After this dream I told it to my sister, Ruth, because I recalled she had buried Catreen with a bottle of her favorite perfume. I did not remember what kind it was. When I told Ruth the dream she said the perfume she put in Catreen's coffin was White Diamond. My mother gave the clue of the perfume, so we could relate the dream to death.

This dream was yet another warning about the possibility of another death in the family. My mother carrying a stick that resembled that of a shepherd's staff was an indication of her guiding whatever situation that was causing darkness in our lives. I know after she died she made it to Heaven and God was using her to help us go through the situations we were facing on earth. Her assignment to prevent the death of her children was revealed in another dream (Dream 6.5).

(Dream 6.3, Golden Clock, 5/25/2007, Jenness)

I am at my mother's house. I am in the small outside room in a meeting with a group of people from work. There is a man of high importance there. I know he just joined the group. He hands out three pictures of himself and his family to pass around. When the pictures are passed around to me I see a picture of a woman, a girl, then one with all three in the family – the man, wife, and child. The one with his family was in a picture frame. The frame is resting down on something.

I pass the pictures to the next person in the room. After everyone is finished looking at the pictures, the man says, "Let us follow our leader,

Tara." I realize I just had a dream about being in Tara's group. I indicate to a lady I have something to tell her. I know I want to tell her about the dream I had.

Everyone gets up and starts to walk outside. I start to walk with them. As I walk, I am looking through my bag for my little notebooks. I find one and look through it to find the dream. I cannot find the dream. I find the other notebook, but the dream is also not in it.

We are walking towards my mother's neighbor, Miss Sally. I have a bottle of water and it falls out of my hand. I wash it off at a standpipe by a mango tree. I am not happy that I did not find the dream, so I can have it as evidence of it being fulfilled. As we walk along, I realize my sister, Petra, is behind me, talking to the crowd about Mall Penn, the district where I grew up. I cannot hear the words she is saying. As we pass through Miss Sally's property, I see my other sister, Ruth. She asks me, "How do you braid hair?" I know she is talking about putting in fake braids. I say to her, "I will show you. You have to part it in three and go under or over."

As we get a little further I notice a tree with oranges on it. I decide to pick a few oranges. When I pick them I realize they are limes. We continue to walk.

I am feeling proud to be showing people my community. I see a mango tree with ripe mangoes. Although I know it is not our property, I decide to pick some of the ripe mangoes to give to a few of the women that were walking with me.

After a while, we seem to be in a room. Ruth is looking around for something. She says, "I cannot find the golden clock. Maybe Kristal gave it to George since he lives nearby. I find myself outside. I look and see an area that is close to where I am standing. I see an entrance to the next property. It is a gold looking gate with one part having a golden looking post and the other part having golden looking fruits.

I find myself back in the room with Ruth, still looking for the clock. I see Petra in her nightgown talking. Her eyes look slightly red because she is upset as she talks. I realize the missing golden clock belonged to Petra. I realize she must be dead why Ruth had said Kristal must have given it away. I say, "Petra, are you dead?" I start to cry, grievously.

This dream was yet another indication of possible death in the family. However, the one to die would make it to Heaven, as indicated by the golden gate and the golden clock. Part of this dream reminds me of another dream I had in which my deceased sister, Elsa, was showing me two clocks (Dream 5.1). That dream's fulfillment was two family members passing away in the same year.

For this dream, it is one clock, for one family member. The clock was golden but there was the suggestion of it been near, as in the golden gate at the adjoining property. The following year, I was faced with many challenging situations in which I came under spiritual attacks. However, God saved me from death.

(Dream 6.4, My Deceased Aunt's Casket, 5/30/2007, Sonia)

I am at a traditional Jamaican setup with singing, eating, and dancing, which usually takes place after someone is dead. It is at my grandmother's house.

I see a casket in front of the house. It is black and has clear glass at the top. I know the casket belongs to my aunt, Catreen, but she is lying on top of it instead of inside. She has on a beige pair of gloves.

I see Nina from my workplace. She says, "Why don't you come and see the body?" I think to myself, "I already see the body. We buried her already. Why are we doing this again?"

Suddenly, I see Aunt Catreen's hand stretched out. She has a stick in her hand that resembles a shepherd's staff. I see that she is getting up. I think to myself, "She is alive. It is a miracle." I go into the house. I see her son, James. I say to him, "Relax, she is alive."

Aunt Catreen comes into the house. She asks me, "Why is James sad?" I say, "Because you were gone. It is OK now." She is wearing a multi-colored sweater.

This is a dream contribution from my daughter, Sonia, and a continuation of the numerous death-related dreams the family had been having. I was not the only one in the family having dreams pointing to death. It is significant that in this dream, Catreen was carrying the stick. It is an indication she too was providing guidance to us, just as in two other dreams in which my mother had a shepherd-looking stick (Dream 6.2; Dream 6.5). My sister had gotten a dream which confirmed that Catreen, like our mother, had made it to Heaven after she died. Also, like my mother, God was using her to help us go through some very rough spiritual battles we were facing (Dream 5.6).

(Dream 6.5, Fight for My Children, 06/08/2007, Donna)

My daughter Zedon, and I go to visit my grandmother. We are outside the house on the lawn. I see my grandmother. She is looking very good. She calls to Zedon saying, "Puss tailer, you are pretty Puss Puss." She then says to me, "I am gone on before to fight for my children because they are going to kill them off. I am still using my Bible and hymn book and I pray." I say to her, "I know you are not leaving that." My grandmother says, "You know I have to use that to conquer the enemy."

She picks up a long stick that looks like the ones used to support vegetation. She walks to the back of the house.

The above dream is a contribution from my niece, Donna. She is one of a few family members who were also given dreams that related to my life. God also used my family to send messages to me in dreams. My mother chose Donna to reveal that her children were faced with the possibility of death and she was on the other side fighting situations for them. My mother had been dead for little over one year. She always liked to read her Bible, sing songs from her hymn book, and pray. It was comforting to know she continued to do the same in her other life. She wanted us to know that reading the Bible, singing songs, and prayers were weapons to be used in fighting the enemy.

This dream with my mother carrying a stick like the one we used to support vegetation was like a staff that a shepherd would carry. I also had a dream in which my mother was carrying a shepherd's staff (Dream 6.2). This dream also served to confirm some of the other dreams my sister, Ruth, and I were having, which pointed to death.

(Dream 6.6, Mother Is Grieving, 7/02/2007, Ruth)

I am at my mother's house. I see a crowd of relatives in my mother's room. I squeeze through the crowd to see what was going on.

When I get in the room, I see my mother bawling (crying out loud) and rolling on the floor in grief, as family members gather around her and watch. I hold her in my hand and say, "Give me six months to deal with it." She replies, "OK."

My sister, Ruth, contributed this dream. My mother was showing Ruth she was fighting the battle in the spiritual world, but Ruth would have to deal with it later, in the physical world. It was fulfilled in the form of my sister, Ruth, taking over from our mother in helping me to fight spiritual battles that became manifested in the physical world.

In January 2008, I had to take shelter at Ruth's house after I was faced with outright spiritual attack at my house. She was of tremendous support while I fought for survival. This is written about in the book, *God's Mission: Spiritual Battles and Revelation of Anti-666*. This is just one of many dreams in which our mother tried to let us know in so many ways, something unusual was going on. Before Catreen died, she gave her the dream about God's herb (Dream 3.7), which was supposed to cure my back problems. However, I later became convinced it was the anti-venom against evil attacks. In two dreams and to two different people, my mother showed us, by the special shepherd's stick, she was providing help and fighting for us (Dream 6.2 & Dream 6.5). This was God's mission for her, on the other side.

(Dream 6.7, Dreams Are About Jenness, 07/15/2007, Ruth)

I see my deceased sister, Catreen. We start talking. She says to me, "I am very happy where I am. I can do anything I want. I can walk through walls." I say to her, "Who is all these dreams about?" She replies, "Jenness."

This dream was contributed by my sister, Ruth. It is very direct in pointing to me as the one who was faced with the possibility of death. The many dreams my family and I were having about death (Dream 6.1 – Dream 6.5; & Dream 7.10) came to realization in outright spiritual attacks which were meant to kill me. This became obvious in January 2008.

We had believed all along that either Ruth or I were going to die, based on our dreams. We had taken out extra life insurances on both of us so that the family would benefit from whichever one of us die. However, with this dream, we concluded it would be me who would die. I spoke to my daughters about this possibility, to prepare them. As it turned out, I did not die, but lived to declare the works God had for me. When I thought I was facing my last moment, God released the song to me, "*I shall not die, but live and declare the works of the Lord, Amen.*" This spiritual incident is written about in my book, *God's Mission: Spirit Battles and Revelation of Anti-666.*

(Dream 6.8, Something Big Is Going to Happen in January, 10/20/2007, Ruth)

I see my sister, Catreen. She says to me, "Something big is going to happen in January."

My sister, Ruth, contributed this dream. It was yet another very clear warning to my family. Since we had had two recent deaths in 2006, we assumed all the warnings from our deceased mother and sister were about someone in the family dying. However, the big thing that happened in January 2008 was the beginning of outright spiritual attacks on me, which is written about in the book, *God's Mission: Spiritual Battles and Revelation of Anti-666*.

Someone hiring others who can cause harm to people, using spiritual means, initiated spiritual attacks against me. At the beginning of these attacks, not knowing how to handle it, I went to a card reader who explained what was happening to me. She told me things I could relate to many of my dreams. Later, I disregarded the help of the card reader as I realized it was only by the power of the Trinity (God, Jesus, and the Holy Ghost [Spirit]) I was able to overcome the tirade of spiritual attacks I had to face.

(Dream 6.9, They Could Have Saved Me, 01/08/2008, Sonia)

I am at Aunt Ruth's house. I look in her bedroom and see Aunt Catreen, who is deceased. She is lying down. I think, "She is dead."

After a while, she turns her head. I can see she is very angry. Still angry, she says to me, "I didn't have to die. They could have saved me."

This dream was contributed by my daughter, Sonia. When she told me this dream I knew Catreen got fed up of trying to tell Ruth and me things in dreams because we were not able to understand well enough. This dream was a desperate attempt by Catreen for us to act on what she and our mother were trying to warn us about. We had just accepted that I would be the one to die. We thought, after all, *"People die when their time come."*

After this dream, Ruth and I decided Catreen was trying too hard to tell us things and we did not understand. We had no idea how to handle the situation. So as not to disappoint her, we decided to check a card reader to get an explanation of what was happening or was going to happen to the family. She explained what was happening to me. What she said, explained some of the dreams we were having. Many of the dreams had to do with spiritual attacks; caused by someone hiring individuals capable of inflicting harm, using evil spirits.

****

We eventually heeded these dream warnings my family and me were having about death. It was only after my sister showed desperation in her dream to Sonia that we acted to enlighten us of the situation. I understand that going to a card reader is not considered to be Christian-like, however, the truth must be told.

At that time, my family and I were used to going to churches that did not speak about spiritual warfare, so we did not have any idea how to handle our situation. It was only after God allowed us to meet the bishop of a Prophetic-type church that we became aware that some churches are equipped to handle spiritual afflictions. Based on my experiences, I believe all churches should address the issue of spiritual afflictions.

Chapter 7

Spiritual Incidents and Attacks

The following dreams about spiritual attacks consist of varied symbolic forms of animals and scenes that are disturbing. In most of these attacks, my defense had been saying a Psalm from the Bible, calling on the name of Jesus, or using prayer.

(Dream 7.1, Lizard Turned into Dog, 9/12/2004, Jenness)

I am at my mother's house. I am in the living room and happen to look at the window. I feel a little scared when I see a small lizard, poising to jump. I know it is unfriendly and I realize I am the intended target. By the time the lizard jumps off the window I quickly move to the side and get out of its way. It disappears. I know it didn't get me.

Soon after this lizard jumps at me, I notice another lizard on the window. This time it is a different kind, Blue Mug. I can tell its intention is to jump off and attack me. I choose not to move but stand where I am. I start to say the 23rd Psalm – "The Lord is my shepherd I shall not want ..." I am more fearful of this lizard. It jumps from the window as I continue to repeat the 23rd Psalm in earnest. I stand my ground because I have the protection of the Lord, my Shepherd.

After jumping off the window the lizard immediately turns into a small white dog with an ugly-looking, small, face. It just stands there and stares at me fiercely. It knows that it cannot touch me. I know that it cannot touch me because I have the protection of the Lord.

This dream took on the Jamaican traditional meaning. Traditionally, a lizard attack means an attack by an enemy. There was a more hostile atmosphere at work towards me after an incident with a co-worker, pointing to me in a staff meeting as being the one who marked down the managers in a performance survey. I subsequently hashed it out with him and his supervisor because I knew I was innocent. He said he was joking.

While I suspect this dream could be applied to situation at work, I had the reassurance that whatever the warning was about, the Lord would be there to protect me. I would not be conquered. Since this dream, I made it a point to say the 23rd Psalm much more often than usual.

(Dream 7.2, The Syringe, 1/18/2007, Jenness)

I am at a place, sitting on a chair. I see a white man dressed in a white lab coat. He has a syringe in his hand, like what a dentist uses. I know he is a doctor, but not a dentist. I can tell he is nervous as he fills and measures medicine in the syringe.

I sit patiently watching and waiting on him. I know he is preparing the syringe for me. He comes to me and injects the syringe in my mouth where my new crown is located. I can feel the fluid going into my gum.

This dream was related to my current situation with dental work. The constant problem I had in this same location with my crown made my dentist seemed incompetent. The crown never seemed to stay in place for more than two weeks. When I told my sister, Ruth, about this dream she asked me if I didn't realize this was a spiritual attack.

My later experience in spiritual warfare, where I had to defend my mouth confirmed this was indeed another means of spiritual attack.

(Dream 7.3, Very Worried on the Other Side, 2/16/2007, Jenness)

I find myself in a car with the contractor, Bill, who is working on my house. He is driving, and I am in the passenger's seat, in the front. He parks the car in the parking lot of a restaurant. He leaves me in the car while he goes into the restaurant. I wait a while for him to come out.

I decide to look to my left. I see the car is parked very close to the edge of a cliff. I feel a little scared. I find myself outside of the car. My deceased sister, Catreen, joins me. I ask, "Are you worried on the other side?" She replies, "Yes. We are very worried on the other side. John and Bill will get the judge channel." I know she is talking about our nephew, John. We start to walk towards the restaurant building.

This dream was a warning that things were going to happen in my life, which my deceased relatives were worried about. As it turned out, things did not work out with Bill. He made several construction errors while doing the job on my house and my husband and I had to get someone else to finish the work. He caused us a lot of financial losses due to wasted material and correction of the work he did, by the architect and other contractors.

The problems with Bill were of a physical nature. I later realized that there were spiritual battles ahead of me which would have caused Catreen and other relatives, on the other side, to be worried about me.

(Dream 7.4, I See Death, 3/12/2007, Jenness)

It is semi-dark. I am walking along a road. I see a dark shadow of a man approaching me. He is not fully formed. He is more like a drawing with black chalk. I can tell he that is "death." I start to scream, "aaaaaaaaaaaaaaah, Jesus!!!"

The scream in the dream was very long and loud. It woke up my daughter and husband. My daughter was sleeping with me. She held onto me and asked, "Mommy what's wrong?" It was about 5:00 a.m. in the morning of March 13, 2007. When I woke up out of the dream I was surprised to see I was alive.

This dream was an attack on my life. It was also an indication that in the face of death, I would call on the name of Jesus, which was encouraging.

(Dream 7.5, Peter Jennings, The Newsman, 4/1/2007, Ruth)

I am at my mother's house. I see my mother cooking in the kitchen. She is cooking dumpling and something else. However, I know it is not enough.

I go to use the bathroom and while I am using it, a reporter shows up to interview my mother. It is as if someone says to me, "That guy is the renowned news broadcaster on ABC." I look and see that it is Peter Jennings. I do not want him to see me since I am using the toilet. I pull the curtain to hide myself. I think to myself, "But, isn't he dead? Oh my God, they still continue what they used to do."

This dream is a contribution from my sister, Ruth. God was also using other family members to alert them of what would be taking place with me.

In 2008, I had undergone many spiritual attacks in which my deceased mother and sister clearly indicated they were helping me to fight the battles. My many noteworthy spiritual experiences no doubt would be newsworthy in real life as well as in life on the other side. This dream from Ruth is showing that Peter Jennings is continuing his work of reporting news, on the other side.

(Dream 7.6, Attack by Snake, 7/20/2007, Jenness)

I am in my mother's house looking up the road through a window. I see my daughter, Sonia, walking down the road. After a while, I see a snake without a head jumps out from the right of the road and throws itself at her. It doesn't land on her but bounces away to the left of the road. Sonia continues to walk down the road. She is not aware that the snake had jumped out at her.

While still at my mother's house looking out the same window, someone says to me, "Tom says you are dead." I think to myself, "He doesn't realize I am not dead.

I next find myself at a place. I am aware that my mother is there with me. I am outside what looks like a housing complex. I see one of the buildings with fogged pane glass along the length of its corridors. The entrance area is made of glass and a light is shining into that entrance.

My mother walks to a part of the corridor and enters the building by pushing her body through the glass. I start to walk to where she is. I intend to push my body through the glass as she had done. From the inside, she points to the glass corridor where the light is shining. I know she means that I should use it and not push my body through the glass, as she did. I walk to the glass corridor where the light shines and enters the building.

Shortly after that, something comes through the glass corridor at a very high speed. We could not figure out what it is until it lands. I look and see it is a large pile of silver wire that is neatly wrapped around a pole. I think to myself, "Since it is electrical wire, why didn't it just come like the lightning?"

This dream was a revelation of a spiritual attack to kill me, not Sonia, as in the dream. Tom expected me to be dead; and me having the idea of going through glass is further confirmation of my intended death, since this is something of which a ghost is capable.

(Dream 7.7, The Lubricant, 7/27/2007, Jenness)

I am in a room. I look at the window and see my mother looking through at me. The two bottom panes of the window are removed. She says to me, "I wrote you long ago."

I go to the window to touch her. She reaches her hand through the window's pane and I hold on to it for a short while. Her hand feels like a live person. I say to her, *"What did you say?"* She starts to talk but I cannot hear what she is saying. She leaves then comes back to the window.

She passes a tube of cream through the window to me. I can see that it is used, and it is a feminine lubricant. I say to her, *"What is this for?"* She says, *"You will be having a lot of sex."* I say, *"With whom?"* She points behind her, *"He is over there."* I look but I don't see the man. I see a crowd of people moving around. I can clearly see two girls walking with the crowd. They are light-skinned and roughly ten-year and twelve-year old. I know that the younger girl is the daughter of the man my mother spoke of.

After a while, my mother comes into the room where I am. This time I am not paying much attention to her. She is looking through some makeup and trying on some foundations. She is talking but I don't hear much of what she is saying. I hear she mentions *"death."*

This was yet another dream that depicts death, in the end. It also revealed spiritual attacks by sexual means, as indicated by the feminine lubricant my mother gave to me, as protection. I was attacked sexually, by spiritual means, during a period of outright spiritual battles from 2008 to 2010.

(Dream 7.8, Crush the Snake, 9/17/2007, Jenness)

I am in a room with some people. I see a very thin snake, about 12" long. Its body is totally covered with very small round beads that are black and white in color. I ignore it since it is not too close to me.

After a while, I see it again. It is partially curled up and not its full length. It comes close to me. I raise my right foot and crush it. I see a part of its body separates and wiggle before it dies. The rest of its body is crushed under my foot.

The next day at work my friend, Donna, called me and told me she had a vision of me being in a cemetery. I was surrounded with many evil spirits. She tried to fight them but could not overpower them. In the vision, she was rebuking and speaking in tongues, but could not manage them all. She had to ask God's angels to fight them. She said the angels told her they would show me a sign of what happened. When I told her about the dream with the snake, she said that was it.

The angels told Donna it was because of my strong faith why evil spirits did not kill me yet. There were a lot of them after me. She told me she did not realize I was going through so much. I asked her if I was able to overcome in the end and she said, "*Yes. The angels conquered the evil spirits.*" She said I was focused on my back problem, but that was a distraction. There were a lot more going on with me.

(Dream 7.9, Lady with Collar Around Neck, 10/23/2007, Jenness)

I am at work walking along the passageway towards my desk. I see my ex-supervisor, Tara. She is walking towards me with a woman. She is holding the woman's hand as if guiding her. The woman has a piece of metal sticking out from one side of her neck. A slim collar around her neck is holding the metal in place.

This was yet another spiritual dream that reveal to me what was being done to me, spiritually. When I sought help from a card reader for spiritual attacks, without telling her about this dream, she told me of someone having a voodoo doll of me with collar around the neck and a stick in it. I must remind the reader here that I went to a card reader to find out what was happening to me because, at the time, I was not aware that there are some churches with anointed people of God who can help with spiritual attacks.

(Dream 7.10, I Am Dead, 11/10/2007, Jenness)

I am on a big bus. A young black girl is driving. As she turns a corner she barely misses an oncoming vehicle. She stands up in the process of swerving the vehicle out of danger. The bus continues along. I see a car stopped across the road, almost blocking our path completely. The driver was able to avoid hitting the car by using the sidewalk to go around it.

The scene changes. I am with my sisters, Petra and Ruth, nieces Berta and Anna, daughters, Kristal and Sonia. We are walking along a road. After a while the road branches into three. I see a lady takes the road on the left. I get the feeling she is my deceased sister, Elsa. The children and I decide to take the road in the middle. We decide to race each other to get to the other side of the road. We start running.

I find myself in a room. I have Anna in my hand, as a six months old baby instead of a fourteen-year-old girl. We are standing in front of a mirror. I turn Anna to face the mirror. After she sees herself in the mirror she gets fearful and makes a scary-looking face for a while. *The fear leaves her face and she looks beautiful. Once again, she looks in the mirror. She becomes fearful and makes a scary-looking face for a while. Once again, the fear leaves her face and she looks beautiful. Petra is beside me, observing what is happening.*

Ruth comes into the room and says to me, "Remember my dream about the frog? It is in the room now in the ceiling." I say, "Lord, it is I." I find myself dead, lying on a bed. I can see Ruth in front of my face. It seems as if she is in another realm. I can hear her say to me, "God be with you." I see a paper with a number, P51160. I know it is my Heavenly number. I am aware Petra is behind me. All along I am saying, "Jesus, Jesus ..." repeatedly.

I woke out of the dream with a headache. This was yet another spiritual attack in which I was supposed to die. As usual, I was calling on Jesus.

This is one dream in which God allowed Ruth to have a similar dream about frog indicating death, the same night. It served to prepare my family and me to be aware that something unnatural is going on within the family.

It was, therefore, no surprise to us when it turned out to be me fighting for my life during many spiritual battles.

God effectively prepared my family to help me go through these spiritual battles and not treat me in the same manner as my older sister, Catreen, who faced similar issues. Her case was treated with purely natural remedies. The outcome for her was a life in and out of the mental hospital and dependency on the government for the remainder of her life.

On the other hand, for me, I was able to overcome all my spiritual battles with the help of a few God-selected family members, a friend, and most of all the Trinity – God, Jesus, and the Holy Ghost [Spirit]. In fact, God has made a business out of my experiences – Works Of Trinity, LLC, and has put me in charge of it for Him, until Jesus Christ of Nazareth returns to take over.

(Dream 7.11, God Is Dancing, 11/17/2007, Jenness)

I am on a land with some family members and others. After a while, we see fires start in one small area of the land after another. We move from each area as soon as a fire breaks out.

We walk until we see a building. The owner of the building lets us in and locks us in a room for safety. We look outside and see small fires are breaking out close behind the building. The air in the room begins to feel stifling. My sister, Petra, and I decide to open the door in the front, slightly to allow fresh air to get in.

A few people coming from the right of the road decide to come into the room for shelter. Soon Petra and I decide we might as well stay outside. We see the amount of small fires continuously increase.

After looking at how helpless the situation is, I say to Petra, "We forgot to pray." My daughter, Kristal, starts to pray. We look in the sky and see the face of God drawn with black chalk. Just then, it starts to rain. God comes down from the sky in the form of a drawn figure of a man in three dimensions and starts to dance around happily. We all stand and watch Him. We know we don't have to worry anymore. The rain is extinguishing the fires.

This dream became reality in outright spiritual attacks in which God came to my rescue. On three occasions, The Holy Spirit within me celebrated with dancing when God allowed me to defeat Satan himself in his attacks on me.

(Dream 7.12, Can't Stay in the House, 11/20/2007, Jenness)

I am at my mother's house in the living room. My niece, Donna, comes to the house. I tell her to stay in one of the front rooms. She goes into the room and sits on the bed with the door open.

My deceased sister, Catreen, comes into the living room. I know she is feeling crazy. I can feel the hazy feeling she has in her head. It reminds me of being in the sun for too long and as a result, you get a hazy simmering feeling. Catreen heads straight to the room where Donna is in. Donna sees her and immediately leaves the room. I know Donna gets scared of staying. I say to her, "You should try and stay. You could stay in the other room." She turns back to go into the room, but again she sees Catreen and get scared. She hurriedly leaves.

This dream exactly allowed me to beforehand experience how I would feel when I was overwhelmed with spiritual attacks. God used Catreen to prepare me ahead of time to know when I should leave my sister's house and seek refuge elsewhere. While going through the situation, I recognized the sensation and the need to leave my sister's house.

(Dream 7.13, Lying Alongside a Tomb, 1/06/2008, Jenness)

I see a Pilipino couple lying on a bed. The husband takes off his underwear and lies on his back. I know the couple is sick. I hear someone says, "It is meningitis." The husband says, "I give it to my wife, so we can both die together."

I find myself in the place of his wife. I am feeling for the husband's testicles. I find three small balls instead of two. The husband's penis was as small as a little child's.

I find myself in a graveyard with the husband. I am lying alongside a tomb with my hand across it. The tomb is very rusty on the top.

For this dream, I got assistance with its interpretation. When I sought help from a card reader she told that me that the individual who initiated spiritual attacks on me had voodoo dolls representing both me and my husband, and they were buried in a cemetery. The voodoo doll representing me was buried beside an old tomb.

This dream had indication of me dying by the infliction of disease, using spiritual mean. The enemy has tried many ways of trying to kill me, by spiritual means. This is just one of them.

(Dream 7.14, Evil Cloud, 1/07/2008, Jenness)

I see a thick dark cloud coming towards me. It is very close to me. I know it is evil. I cry out, "Jesus, Jesus, Jesus..." repeatedly.

I woke up calling the name of Jesus. The noise I was making woke up my husband and daughter. My daughter rushed from her room and asked me what happened. This was yet another spiritual attack meant to do me harm.

(Dream 7.15, The Surgery, 4/15/2008, Jenness)

I am in a room. I see my husband as a small baby in a glass cage. I know he is going to have a surgery to remove something from his groin area. I see a male doctor and two female nurses.

The doctor has a very small hacksaw in his hand. I do not see him perform the surgery, but I soon see him with a cut of beef in his hand. The cut is slightly jagged. The two nurses are not pleased with the surgery. One of them turns to me and shows me two neatly cut slices of pork loins. She says, "He should have done it like this."

The next day while walking, I felt pain in my right leg and strain in the right side of my belly. I realized the surgery I dreamt about was a spiritual surgery performed on me and not my husband.

****

The lesson in my spiritual dream experiences is that you need to be watchful of dreams with unusual situations and animal forms. God will show you what is being done to you spiritually, so you can be warned. God first used my mother and sister to give my family and I dreams, warning of my possible death before spiritual attacks were launched at me in my dreams. Spiritual dreams are sometimes not just warnings of things to come, but are actual attacks on your life. Your enemy will attack you spiritually, in your dreams, as a way of trying to hurt or even kill you. The dream patterns in this chapter serve as examples of this.

In the above dreams about spiritual attacks, I became aware of when I was being attacked spiritually only because my spirit had become awaken. We all possess a spirit as a part of being a human. We were created from a Spiritual being, God, Who gave us each a spirit to communicate with Him in spirit.

Satan, who himself is a spirit, was cast out of Heaven with his followers (Revelation 12:7-12). We are faced with attacks from Satan, his followers, and those who access his powers to inflict harm on others, through spiritual means. As indicated in my dreams, they can all be overcome with the name of Jesus.

Chapter 8

Sally's Struggles with Illness

Sally was a co-worker who suffered from sarcoidosis and bronchiectasis disease. Sarcoidosis is an autoimmune disease which causes inflammation in the lymph nodes, lungs, liver, eyes, skin, heart, brain. These areas are damaged with significant amounts of scar tissue. The scar tissue inhibits normal functions. Bronchiectasis is a disease of the bronchial tubes (PubMed Health).

After my dream about my two pregnant coworkers was fulfilled (Dream 2.1), she bothered me often to dream about her. I told her it didn't just happen like that – upon request. However, I was deeply touched by her suffering, as I too was suffering from back problems.

Once I started dreaming about Sally, I had some amazing dreams about her; some of which have been fulfilled already.

(Dream 8.1, Leading Co-worker Through Forest, 01/16/2005, Jenness)

I am walking on a road when I become aware that there is a large wolf behind me. I know it intends to hurt me. Suddenly, the road becomes very steep and winding downwards. I continue to walk down the road but the wolf behind me cannot manage the downward steep of the road. It rolls off the road into a precipice on the left. I am very relieved the wolf is gone. After that, the road suddenly ends with nothing but forest in front of me.

I start to follow a narrow path in the forest. Soon after that, a much smaller harmless wolf comes up beside me, trying to get fed. I keep squeezing water into its mouth from a bottle. It is always jumping up for more. I am juggling between feeding the small wolf while keeping focus on finding the path to a way out of the forest.

I come to a clear area in the forest and see a few oranges on the ground. I decide to peel one and give it to the small wolf. Another small animal joins it. That animal also wants to be fed. I feed both with the orange. They both disappear after getting the orange. I am relieved to see them go.

Soon after the animals left I hear Sally from a distance says, "Why didn't you wait for me?" I can tell she is coming down the same road I came from. I reply, "I didn't know you were coming." Sally joins me in the forest. I continue to try and find the way out of the forest.

Shortly after that, my husband joins us. As I continue to try and find my way out of the forest my husband keeps on complaining, "You shouldn't have come this way if you didn't know your way out." Sally doesn't complain at all. I keep ignoring my husband's complaints. I feel extremely determined to find my way out of the forest. I know Sally is just as determined as she follows behind me all the way. Although there is not much light, I clear my way through thick bushes and trees. At all times I lead, while Sally and my husband follow behind.

I eventually find a track. I follow it. It leads us to a main road. My husband was no longer with us. Sally and I feel very happy we are finally out of the forest. I recognize that the main road is the one in the community where I grew up. I say to Sally, "I am a little closer to my house than yours." She turns to the right to go up the road while I turn to the left to go down the road to my mother's home.

In this dream, God revealed to me that someone meant me harm and both Sally and I would eventually make it out of our shared struggle of balancing the demands of work along with fighting ongoing illnesses. God also showed me to ignore my husband's complaints as I struggle to make my way out of my situation. He was always complaining about one thing or the other. My back problem affected the level of care and attention I could give to my family. Understandably, he was frustrated with the situation. However, his constant complains did not help it.

I had this dream while I was out of work due to my back problems. I emailed Sally and mentioned I had a dream about her. She was anxious to hear about it. By this time, I had gained the respect of my co-workers as a true dreamer, since the dream I had about the two pregnant co-workers came true. I sent her an email relating the dream.

This dream meant that both Sally and I would make it out of our troubles. For Sally, her struggles ended when she died. For me, it is making it through one series of spiritual attacks after another; all of which served to take me to higher levels of anointing in God.

When I went back to work and was talking to Sally she said what was strange about the dream was that when her mother was pregnant with her she was living in a house outside the military base in Germany and she would often walk in the black forest. The dream really had something in it that caught her attention.

(Dream 8.2, Praying for Sally, 5/6/2006, Jenness)

I am at work. I go to the computer lab and I see Sally. I go and sit beside her. I know she is not feeling well. I say to her, "Are you OK?" She said, "No." She shows me her right hand. I see it is swollen.

I say to Sally, "I will pray for you." I start to pray to God to heal her. The prayer is emotionally deep. I can literally feel the emotion. It is one of deep sorrow and pain.

This dream was fulfilled. The day after the dream Sally did not show up at work. When she came back to work I told her about the dream. She told me her right hand was really swollen. That was one of the symptoms of the disease she had. It took a while for the swelling to go down, after continuing with medication.

(Dream 8.3, Feminine Pads for Sally, 1/9/2007, Jenness)

I am ready to go to work. I pass by a mirror. I look in the mirror and see I am dressed but my hair isn't combed. I comb my hair.

I find myself at work. I see Sally and tell her I had almost come to work without combing my hair. She asks, "Do you have any pads?" I know she is talking about feminine pads. I reply, "Follow me." She follows me to a building. I use my badge to scan us in. The building is mostly empty. I take her to a drawer. I open the bottom drawer and show her where I keep my feminine pads.

Just before this dream, I went to bed praying to God to heal Sally. I watched her suffer constantly with sarcoidosis attacking one area of her body after another. We usually encourage each other, as we were both battling illnesses.

I decided to carry some feminine pads to work just in case Sally should ask me for some. When I got to work, I put them in a bottom drawer.

While at work, we had a team meeting that lasted for about two hours. During the meeting, I told Sally I had something to tell her. Around lunchtime, I got the opportunity to tell her the dream. She asked, "*Are you serious?*" I replied, "*Yes.*" She asked, "*Is it sanitary pads?*" I replied, "*Yes.*" She said, "*My period started just two hours ago. I could feel the discomfort while in the meeting.*" I told her to walk with me to my desk because I brought some pads, just in case. She told me she was planning on going out lunchtime to buy pads. I gave her some of what I brought to work.

Just as the feminine pad is an absorbent material, God has shown me in this dream I should help Sally by absorbing some of the pain she was feeling due to her disease. I had been trying the best I could to counsel and encourage her, but I knew she was going through a tremendous amount of distress.

(Dream 8.4, Looking for Medicine, 1/15/2007, Jenness)

I am in the Bronx with my co-worker, Sally. The area is where I used to live. It looks somewhat rundown. It is semi-dark because it is night, but there are some streetlights. The road is very muddy and has gravel in some areas. Sally is walking around, going in and out of one building after the other. She is looking for her medicine. I get the impression she doesn't know exactly what she is looking for. I follow her around patiently.

There are some people watching us, as we walk around. I get the feeling they are drug addicts, since it is late in the night. Sally totally ignores them. I feel she is determined to find her medicine. After going to one building, I wait outside, just as patiently as before for her. This time she comes out with two ice cream popsicles and gives one to me. It is vanilla with orange and chocolate fudge down the middle. I eat the popsicle just as a child would after an ice cream truck visits.

Sally walks to another area where there is more light. There are people hanging around. They are watching us too. One young guy comes up to us and asks for money. As Sally reaches for her purse I say, "I have some change." I reach into my pocket and get some change. I give him the coins. He walks away. Sally continues along the road and I continue to follow her.

The scene changes, Sally and I are still in the Bronx. We are in the area where she first started to look for her medicine. This time the road is not muddy or full of gravel. It is paved and has no sign of ruts. I find myself with a large metal sieve. I know I just *washed it. I walk along the road towards Sally. I hand her the sieve when I am close enough to her. I know she understands it means she should use it to strain her medicine.*

This dream reflected Sally's situation, my desire to help her, and my patience in counseling her through her illness. She had been to so many doctors, trying to get help for her sarcoidosis disease, but it just continued to attack one part of her body after another. She even went to a doctor who was doing research on sarcodosis disease to try a new medicine. In the end, it did not work out with this doctor and she started seeing a different one.

At work, I told Sally about the dream, she asked me to describe the ice cream popsicle in the first part of the dream. When I described it to her she was immediately very curious. She said her favorite ice cream popsicle, as a child, fitted the description. As a child, she would only buy that kind of ice cream popsicle from the ice cream truck. Her mother would buy it for her when she was upset to calm her down.

(Dream 8.5, Breathing Not Helped, 06/7/2007, Jenness)

I am at a place that reminds me of the Bronx. I am with a crowd of people walking on the road, under the subway. A female police officer comes and starts to direct us where to walk and cross each intersection on the road. The police officer gets us across one light, then stops us and says, "I have to cross the next group of people."

We wait until the police officer comes back. She says, "I have to be doing many things at the same time. I have to cross this group, the other group, and I have to use my baton." She touches her baton as she mentions it. She takes us across another stop light.

The scene changes; I find that I am in a building with the same police officer and some people. The police officer says, "I have to check my breathing." She goes to the wall and pulls out a long tube with a long and narrow plastic container, filled with clear liquid at the end. She takes the container and squirts it in her mouth once. She made a coughing sound. She puts back the container and then walks away.

Sally comes up and squirts the container in her mouth. She did not make the coughing sound. She squirts it again, but again she did not make the coughing sound. I can tell she is concerned about this. I ask Sally, "Is this good?" she replies, "No." She walks away. I feel deeply concerned for her.

A few months after this dream, Sally's sarcoidosis disease progressed in her lungs and ever since she started coughing constantly. At times, we would know she was at work just by hearing the constant coughing, nearby.

(Dream 8.6, Co-worker Feeling Sick, 9/22/2007, Jenness)

I am at work. I see my co-worker, Sally, who was on disability at the time. She comes up to me looking very sick in the face. She says, "I am feeling very sick. I am going home."

I say to Sally, "Wait. I will drive you home in your car. Just wait until I find someone to follow us, so I can get a ride back." I feel concerned about her. I look around and see our co-worker, Juan, sitting in the lab. I think of asking him to drive his car and follow us.

The following day I called Sally at her home to tell her the dream. She told me she too had a dream about us, two days before. She dreamt, she came back to work and sat at her desk. She started feeling very sick. She then went to the computer lab to look for me. She saw a Spanish co-worker and me in the lab. She told me she was sick and had to leave. She went to the front entrance by Human Resources. As she opened the door she saw only very bright light.

Sally's dream was very similar to mine. The very bright light in her dream is symbolic of death. God gave us similar dreams, so Sally would pay close attention to the dreams I was having of her. She felt sick one day after coming back from disability and had to go home. However, I did not have to drive her home.

(Dream 8.7, She Had Enough Faith, 10/18/2006, Jenness)

I am at a place with a crowd of people, sitting and watching a fashion show. After several ladies come out and modeled, I recognize the last one. She is Esta Gonsalves, a former co-worker from a company I used to work for.

After she finishes down the runway, she meets me where I am sitting. I am very happy to see her. I feel happy she had the faith to achieve this.

I am so overwhelmed with joy for Esta that I start to cry. While I am crying I become aware Sally is there. She is complaining to a guy saying, "She never believed I had enough faith to make it through." I know Sally is talking about me.

God was showing me the level of faith Sally had in dealing her difficulties. I got the feeling I was supposed to help her get through her illness but at times I was wondering if she had enough faith in God to accept that He would heal her. She would often say God would heal her, when He is ready.

****

I know these dreams about Sally were not in vain. As in the dream about leading Sally through the forest, I was supposed to lead her to the healing God planned for her. Unfortunately, I was not able to carry out this mandate. Sally left work after it became too much to cope with work and her illness. I was in touch with her occasionally and promised to give her a copy of this book, when I was done with it. I did not expect her to die suddenly from heart attack.

It was sad for me to hear of her death. It reminded me of the sudden death of my sister, Catreen, after we had made big plans to visit Jamaica to investigate a dream she had about me. With Catreen sudden death, I knew I had to be exceptionally strong in my fight against spiritual wickedness. With Sally's death, I know I must be highly courageous in my *"end-time"* ministry of saving souls and not think that I have time. I kept putting of calling her, wanting to be able to tell her that I was done with the book, when we talk. Sally's soul is with God and her death will be a constant reminder to me to not put off matters of the soul. I know that a part of my end-time ministry will be to proclaim an urgent need for repentance to bring about salvation, so that souls can make it to Heaven.

Chapter 9

Stand-alone Dreams

The following are interesting dreams that seem to stand on their own. Stand-alone dreams are just as significant as those that link to form a story, since they too have been fulfilled, or have the markings of something important to watch. Many of them have been fulfilled; some in relative ways, and few are revelations.

(Dream 9.1, Cops Looking for Husband to Arrest Him, 02/12/2004, Jenness)

I am a street, close to my home. I notice a few cops. I somehow become aware that they are looking for my husband to arrest him.

After having this dream, I told my husband about it and warned him to be careful because by then we saw my dream about two pregnant co-workers came true (Dream 2.1). As usual, he dismissed what I said to him. At the time of the dream he had a situation where he was scheduled to go to court for a speeding ticket. He got a lawyer to represent him.

My mother-in-law was sick, and my husband planned on going to visit his mom but was waiting to get a court date. He eventually decided to purchase his ticket without receiving word on a set court date. It so happened that just a few days before his departure date, he got his court date. The date coincided with when he would be out of the country for two weeks. His lawyer assured him it would not be a problem. He would reschedule the court date.

The court date came and passed while my husband was out of the country. A few days after the court date passed I got a letter from the court for my husband. It was a warning that a warrant was out for his arrest, due to his non-appearance in court. I reminded him of my dream. His lawyer was able to straighten out the situation and he avoided an arrest.

This dream came true within a fairly short period of time. After that situation, my husband began to pay more attention to my dreams.

(Dream 9.2, Opened Window, 07/12/2004, Jenness)

I am at my mother's house sleeping in her bed. The bed is against the window and the window is wide opened. While I am sleeping a dark-skinned lady came by the window. I do not recognize her. She starts urging me to get up. She says, "Jenness, Jenness, wake up and close the window". She repeats this many time, with urgency. The anxiety in her voice gets to me.

In the dream, I am thinking I really must get up; otherwise, something will happen through the window. I am feeling totally exhausted, but I start to struggle with myself to get up. As I am struggling to get up, the lady goes away. Physically and mentally, I can fell the exhaustion and determination to wake up. I want to get up to close the window. I can feel myself waking up.

I thank God for sending someone to wake me up, just in time. Towards the end of the dream, I eventually struggled out of my sleep with the real feeling of exhaustion to find the house in total darkness. I awoke from my nap after a long day at work. I was alone in the house; my family was on vacation. I got out of the couch and turned on the living room light. I then checked the adjoining dining room window. It was wide opened.

It was a hot day and before falling asleep on the couch I had opened the window in the dining room all the way up. I quickly closed it. I decided to make sure all other windows were closed.

I turned on the outside light and went down the basement to check the windows. The windows were slightly opened, and I closed those as well. The doorbell rang. I was feeling scared, considering the dream I just had and the fact I was alone in the house. The bell rang once more. I decided to ask, "*Who is it?*" A male voice responded from the side of the house where the outside light shone.

From the basement window I could see that it was a white male, slight to medium built. He was carrying something in his hand that was more like a piece of cardboard. He was wearing a green shirt and khaki pants. According to where I was in the basement, I could partially see from the window, but he wouldn't be able to see me. He said, "*Domino's Pizza. Is this 1185?*" I replied, "*Wrong number.*" The man walked away. Whatever was in his hand did not look like a pizza box. If he was looking for house number 1185 then he should have been going down the street, according to the street numbering. Furthermore, the house number was at the door where he rang the bell.

This was yet the most powerful and immediate fulfillment of a dream I had. I woke up just in time to close the window that was wide opened, inviting potential criminals to come in. A crime of opportunity was avoided due to the lady in the dream urging me to close the window. To this day, I don't believe that man was a pizza deliveryman.

(Dream 9.3, Checks Falling from The Sky, 03/23/2005, Jenness)

My sister, Ruth and I are in an opened space at somewhere unfamiliar to us. There was nobody else around. Somehow, I become aware there is a bank robbery. After that awareness, I happen to look up in the sky and see a small plane flying low. Suddenly, a part of the plane opens up and checks start to fall out – lots of them. Ruth and I start picking them up. We take them to the bank. I somehow become aware one million dollars is missing.

This dream was fulfilled in a relative way. Although there was no robbery I was chosen to intervene to prevent it. I found a lot of money while in my credit union.

In May 2006, I went to my credit union to do a few transactions, which included depositing checks and withdrawing money. The money envelopes were behind the cashier counter, in front of the customer. I reached to pick up an envelope from the stack. I noticed a very bulky envelope. I picked it up and saw that it contained a lot of dollar bills. I couldn't count them all at first glance. I could easily have taken it, but instead, I decided to hand the envelope with money to the cashier. I knew he might be able to identify the owner. After the cashier checked the money he told me it was ten thousand dollars. Since I had a few transactions to do I was with the cashier for quite a while.

Later, a Chinese man came up to the cashier while I was still at the counter. He asked if he left some money there. He seemed anxious. The cashier pointed to me and told the man I found the money. He merely told me thanks and took the money from the cashier. Someone else might have shown more gratitude.

(Dream 9.4, Hit in the Back, 10/5/2005, Jenness)

I am in the back of a car and my sister, Ruth, is driving. I physically feel an impact as if the vehicle is hit in the rear. I ask Ruth, "Did we get hit?" She says, "Yes." She stops the car. We get out and look at the back of the car. There is slight impact mark. Ruth gets back into the driver's seat and starts driving. But, this time her driving is uncontrolled. I start feeling afraid because I can see she no longer has the confidence she needs to drive.

I am relieved when she makes a stop where a few roads merge. I can tell she is uncertain of what to do. I take the opportunity and quickly jump into the driver's seat. I turn the car onto the correct road and keep on driving.

Certain aspects of this dream were fulfilled in a relative way. The car in the dream was related to Ruth's house and the accident was incidents she had with her house during the winter of 2005.

I was staying at Ruth's house when there were two consecutive days of below zero temperatures during the second week of December 2005. This caused frozen pipe and cracked water meter. Although she had to call her regular maintenance man and 311 for emergency help, I was there to help her through it. At one point, I had to take control of the situation when additional problems of leaky steam pipe and broken pipe valve problem occurred, and Ruth told me she couldn't deal with it.

Ruth was certainly not driving a car, but she was driving her house's affairs when she got hit with excessive use of oil, frozen pipes, unstoppable running water, and leaky steam pipe. I took control of the situations and was able to get the household affairs under control. Ruth felt less stressed after I took over. After all the dilemmas were over I told her about the car accident dream I had about her. She immediately said my dream was about the house problems, which she couldn't handle, and I stepped in and took control.

(Dream 9.5, One Dollar Bargain, 12/23/2005, Jenness)

I am in a Lowes store. I am looking to buy a refrigerator. I am aware that my husband is somewhere in the store. I decide on the refrigerator I want to buy. The salesman writes up the invoice for $5004. He somehow leaves me with the invoice.

Another salesman comes along and tells me, "The other salesman did not give you the discount you should get since you bought a refrigerator here more than four years ago." He takes the invoice from me and looks at it. He says, "I will adjust the price." He writes down $5000 subtracts from $5004. He then turns to me and says, "You only have to pay $1. I looked more closely at the invoice and say to myself, "He made a mistake. I should pay $4."

Certain aspects of this dream were fulfilled. I came across a surprising one-dollar bargain. The Lowes store in the dream was related to the pharmacy where I got the one-dollar bargain, in real life.

The morning after this dream, I went to a nearby strip mall. I ended up looking at perfume gift sets for Christmas. The qualities were good and so were the prices. I bought about fifteen gift sets. After I left the pharmacy and went to my vehicle, I realized I did not have any wrappings paper for my presents.

I decided to go back into the pharmacy to buy a roll of wrapping paper. I ended up selecting a small roll that didn't have a price tag and took it to get a price check. The cashier said it was not coming up with any price and asked how much I wanted to pay. I said, "*A dollar.*" To my surprise, the cashier rang up the wrapping papers for only one dollar. Of course, I was very happy to get that price.

The dollar bargain was a fulfillment of this dream. After going back to the pharmacy, I bought wrapping paper for the very low price of $1, just like the salesman in the dream told me I had to pay because I had purchased there before. The twist was that I offered to pay $1 for my purchase, not the other way around. I found myself in a position where I was able to control the fulfillment of this dream. Sometimes the dreamer has the power to control the dream's fulfillment.

(Dream 9.6, Out of Gas, 1/1/2006, Jenness)

I am driving my van. It isn't clear to me which road I am on, but I know that I need gas. I keep passing by each gas station, thinking I will get gas at the next one.

After a while, the van stops. There is a little steam coming from the hood. My husband seems angry with me. He asked, "Why did you let it run out of gas?"

Although I did not have steam from my van's hood and I did not exactly run out of gas, I had an incident in which I kept passing by each gas station, thinking I would get gas at the next one.

The next day after this dream, I was driving from New York to New Jersey. My gas tank was less than a quarter full, but I figured that should be able to take me across to New Jersey where gas prices were lower. There were a few gas stations along my route. I planned to buy gas as soon as I came across the first one. However, the first gas station I came across had a price of $2.25 for regular. I was upset that the price rose from $2.19, just a few days ago.

I decided I would continue to the next gas station. That station too had a price of $2.25 and so did the next five gas stations along the route. In the meantime, my gas tank was getting lower as I continued to search for a better price. When the gas tank was about one-eighth full, I decided I would have to buy gas at the next gas station. I had no choice now, since I was cutting it close. The *"empty"* light would come on any moment and I was on the highway. When I pulled up at the next gas station, the price was $2.19. I was satisfied.

Luckily for me, unlike in the dream, I did not run out of gas. The dream was just an indication of the situation in which I would find myself. I could recognize when I was in the situation, but I had enough gas in the gas tank to take such a chance.

(Dream 9.7, Worker Is Sick, 5/30/2006, Jenness)

I wake up to the smell of stinking cigar. I think to myself, "Bunny must be here already." I go down to the basement. There I see Bunny on a stepladder with a hammer, trying to nail something through the beam in the ceiling.

I can tell Bunny is feeling weak. I watch him for a while. He eventually falls forward. I catch him before he touches the floor.

I can see a lot of mucus coming from Bunny's nose. After he recovers, I go and get one of the dusk masks I have around the house. I give it to Bunny and tell him to wear it while he works. He doesn't take it but decides to wear a yellow plastic bag, hanging over his face. He later changes it to his own dusk mask. I start to help him to do the work.

After a while, he goes to another area to work. He lets out a very huge sneeze. A man working nearby steps away to avoid breathing in Bunny's germs. I also step away. I realize Bunny gets better after that very huge sneeze.

Bunny was a worker at my house who had difficulty finishing the work he was contracted to do, due to illness. He was sick with allergy, which contains mucus. He came to work one day when another contractor was there, working. Bunny felt sick and had to leave early. The sneeze in the dream was related to Bunny's allergy that flared up.

For the past two and one-half weeks Bunny had been telling us that he was very sick with allergies. We were not sure if we should believe him.

My interpretation of this dream was that God was showing me Bunny was truly sick. We had seriously doubted the extent of his illness. I had planned to file a formal complaint against him. However, God intervened and showed me that he was truly sick.

This dream was fulfilled. The evening following the dream Bunny called me and said he was at my house. He said he tried to work but was in such pain he had to leave. He would try to come back the next day to work. I told him about my dream and asked him to wear a mask while working to prevent aggravation of his allergies. The next time he came to work he brought his prescription to prove he was sick.

(Dream 9.8, Help Me Win the Lottery, 11/24/2006, Jenness)

I am at my sister, Ruth's, house. I go into a room. I see my deceased sister, Catreen, hiding behind the door. She has a full figure; like when she was alive. I know she is dead. I say to her, "Catreen, can you help me win the lottery? Remember how hard we were working on it? Remember, we also have James to take care of. If you need help you can ask Ansa."

Catreen doesn't reply to me. She is acting shy and uncertain. She goes to the electrical panel in the room and starts to blow away the dust. I get the impression that is all she wants to focus on.

This dream reflected my desire. Catreen had died less than a month before this dream. Before Catreen died, we were both playing a few sets of numbers for the lottery, based on a dream she had.

(Dream 9.9, Protecting My Daughter, 1/31/2007, Jenness)

I am at my mother's house. I realize someone is killed. I am thinking, "It wasn't me because I was not around when it happened. I walk towards the house. I see my mother. She says to me, "Ronald will know about it." We both walk to Ronald's house, which is neighboring her property. Ronald joins us. We walk back to my mother's house. My mother takes us into the outside room to talk.

Before we start talking, Rashad, a co-worker, comes into the room, unannounced, to get something. I am thinking, "I thought he was finished with this room." He leaves. My mother and neighbor also leave.

My younger daughter, Sonia, comes into the room. I know she is hiding from someone. I lay on top of her to protect her. Then, I saw a young fair-skinned girl at the door. I realize she is the one out to get my daughter. She cannot come inside. She leaves. I then realize the fuss was about some clothes my daughter purchased at the Macy's store. I take the clothes and decide I will return them.

Although someone was not killed, my daughter later reported to me she was having serious problems with her roommate in college. Sonia's roommate was a fair-skinned girl.

Roughly two weeks after this dream, I got a call from Sonia. She said she was having problems with her roommate. They just went through a round of cursing each other out. The roommate had come back from the winter break with a different attitude. Sonia decided that she was going to take up the matter with the Resident Assistant and the Residence Director.

I talked Sonia through dealing with the situation. I reminded her of the dream and told her we were warned of the upcoming situation, so she shouldn't take it too hard. God was looking out for her. In the end, my daughter was able to cope better with the roommate after taking the matter to a higher authority.

(Dream 9.10, Thrown Over by Ice, 2/15/2007, Ruth)

My sisters, Jenness, Petra, and I are by a large body of water. It looks more like the ocean. I see a whale-looking thing in the water. It has a very long tail that projects out of the water. It starts floating towards Jenness. It becomes more like a big garbage bag full of ice, as it gets closer. When it is close to Jenness it bursts open with a lot of ice spilling outwards. The force knocks Jenness over and throws her into the water.

I start yelling, calling out to Petra to come and help me with Jenness. It is as if she is not breathing. Petra and I get blankets; wrap Jenness in them and try to revive her. We keep trying until she finally comes around.

This is a dream contribution from my sister, Ruth, about me. God gave to Ruth this dream so that other family members could be aware something was going to happen to me. There was an incident with ice breaking up although it did not knock me over. However, it frightened me. The whale-looking thing in the water in the dream was related to my van with ice on top of it.

Stand-alone Dreams

On February 16th, 2007, I left work during my lunch break to go to the post office. On my way there, I had to make a left turn at a light. Suddenly, it seemed out of nowhere, enough ice fell on my van's windshield to completely obstruct my vision. I was very frightened. The amount of ice was too much to continue driving. I stopped and put on my hazard lights. As the Lord would have it, the vehicles behind were far enough to stop in time.

I came out of the van and removed the ice from the front windshield before continuing to the post office. At the post office, I checked the top of the van and saw more ice was melting. I took the time to cautiously clean it off this time. God had saved me from what could have been a more dangerous situation.

Another possible interpretation of this dream is the fact that in 2008, I had to seek refuge at Ruth's house after constant spiritual attacks on me, at my house because too much. Ruth sought the assistance of Petra in helping me. Thanks to their help, I survived it all to write about my experiences.

(Dream 9.11, Show Me the Guy, 3/23/2007, Jenness)

It is nighttime. I am passing by a gym. I think to myself, "I want God to show me the guy." After I speak, a beam of light starts to pass over people at different areas of the gym, while they exercise. As the light pass over the individuals, I can see them clearly. The light stops at a group of guys. It focuses on three guys I recognize are from my high school.

The three guys walk away to come to me. One is left behind and two come to me. One is dark in color and the other is brown in color. The brown-colored guy's name is Evert Powell. The other guy is his high school friend, Kevin Baxter, who is short in statue. Close up, I can see Evert has aged. He says to me, "I want to have sex with you now." I laugh and ask, "Do you have any children?" He replies, "I have four."

Kevin leaves us. I walk with Evert along the road. We seem to be going somewhere. My daughter, Sonia, joins us. She says, 'I want to go to the library." I say, "No."

Evert Powell is a high school classmate I had a crush on, although I did not tell him about it. Since January of 2011

I began to see the fulfillment of this dream as God used the profile of Evert and other means to "*show me the guy.*"

(Dream 9.12, The Plain Tomb, 8/27/2007, Jenness)

My sisters, Ruth and Petra, and I are in the middle of a burial ground. I know it is where my mother is buried. We are walking among the tombs. I see a plain stone tomb without a name. It is turned cross ways and not facing the same direction as the others. I say to Ruth, "Whose tomb is this?" She replies, "I don't know whose it is, but the body was sent to me by mistake. I have to hide it from Ansa."

After she says this, we could feel the angry spirit of Ansa. Petra and I try to focus our efforts in protecting Ruth from Ansa's spirit. After it fades, I find myself with an avocado in my hand. I know it is partially ripe. Petra takes the avocado from me and tears off a piece. She further breaks that piece into three pieces and gives them to Ruth to spread around the crossway tomb.

This dream was related to the destruction of our uncle, Jossy's, tomb during a hurricane. A tree fell on the tomb and did significant damage to it. The most interesting thing about this dream was that the same night, Ruth also had a dream about tomb and our mother, Ansa.

(Dream 9.13, I Win the Lottery, 12/05/2007, Jenness)

I look in my handbag and take out a sheet of paper. It has the lottery numbers I play sometimes.

Next, I am in a grocery store. I find myself with lottery tickets. I go up to the cashier, who is Indian. I look to the left and see a poster board with the lottery jackpot. It is over seven million dollars. I give my lottery tickets to the cashier to check. He checks them. I realize I win the lottery. I also realize that six other people win. I start to calculate in my head that I will get over one million dollars.

A few other people in the store realize I win the lottery. They start to get interested in me. A cousin called Bounty Boy comes up to me. I know he wants to share in the lottery winnings with me. I start to hurry and sign all my lottery tickets because I am thinking someone might want to steal them from me.

I see my sister, Ruth, in the store. I know we both win the lottery. She comes up to me and we both walk to another room and sit on a bench. I see there are a folded paper and her lottery ticket in her coat pocket. I am thinking someone can easily steal them. I say to her, "Put them in your purse."

About five days before the dream I was looking for a cousin's phone number which I knew I wrote down somewhere. I decided to look in the bag I was travelling around with while I was in Jamaica. I could not find the phone number, but I came across a piece of paper with the lottery numbers my sisters, Ruth and Catreen, and I played sometimes. The numbers were based on a dream Catreen had before she died. Finding the lottery numbers in my handbag was confirmation of the dream. However, I am still waiting on the fulfillment of this dream.

****

Each of the above dreams tells a story of its own, except for the two related to me winning the lottery. The dreams I share in this chapter give further insights into different dream contents and interpretations.

Chapter 10
Work-related Dreams

This collection of dreams is work-related. Some of them were fulfilled. At times, the fulfillments come with comical twists; however, the relationships are clear.

Although things got rocky on the job at times, I had the special knowledge that God cares deeply about me. He was providing me with guidance in dreams which made me feel special within. This was more fulfilling than feeling special without, based on mankind interactions.

(Dream 10.1, Disabled Co-worker, 09/14/2001, Jenness)

I am at work. I see my co-worker, Sammy, walking with a walker. It is the half-round type, which older people use to get around when having difficulty walking. The steps of the building are altered to provide easy access for the walker.

Sammy later fractured his hip while running in the New York Marathon. The walker in the dream was related to the crutch Sammy returned to work with, after he had been out on disability.

At the time of this dream, I didn't pay much attention to it. I merely mentioned it to another co-worker, Razan. After Sammy got injured, Razan reminded me of my dream about him.

(Dream 10.2, Co-worker Pointing Me Out, 01/07/2004, Jenness)

I am at my mother's house. I see a group of guys coming towards the house. I realize that they are going from house to house looking for people. They are a group of terrorists belonging to Bin Laden. One of my co-workers, Dave, is with them. I decide to hide from them.

I go in one of my mother's bedrooms to hide. Dave sees me going there. He points to me telling the bad guys, "She is hiding in that room." They come to get me.

Certain aspects of this dream have been fulfilled. There was an incident where Dave was pointing to me. In a relative way, the bad guys were the managers in real life.

Based on the dream, I didn't expect my co-workers to be associated with those infamous bad guys, but I got the feeling the dream was a warning for me to be wary of Dave.

A couple of months following this dream we had a group meeting to hear the results of our yearly survey. The top-level manager went over the results question by question. One of the managers commented on the result of each question. He said the team of managers needed to understand the issues in certain areas.

As he read the result of one question one of my co-workers, Dave, said, "*I know who did that*," and pointed to me. I was very upset because he did not know who gave what ratings. I responded to Dave's accusation immediately in the meeting. I was upset that he tried to create a bad image of me in the eyes of the managers. That was the moment when I remembered this dream. Dave was this same coworker who was pointing me out to the bad guys in the dream. These managers were far from being in the same categories as those bad guys, but the dream's fulfillment came to me in a comical way. It was close enough to this reality.

(Dream 10.3, First Moving to Another Group, 10/20/2004, Jenness)

I am at work. I see my supervisor, Tara. I know she is currently on maternity leave. She is walking towards the conference room our group uses regularly. I suddenly realize she is moving to another group. I am thinking, "Why did they move her while she is on maternity leave?"

I then realize I am also leaving to another group and will be working with James, a co-worker who recently left my group. I realize I will be working on a legacy system and I will be getting paid more. I see my new boss. She is walking away from me, so I cannot see her face. She is tall, slim, and has very blonde hair.

Shortly after Tara moved me to another group, she later moved to a different group. I got the highest pay raise since working with the company, after I move to the new group. The new boss I started working with used to work in the same group as James and fitted the description of the new boss I dreamt about.

Tara was one of the co-workers I dreamt of being pregnant (Dream 2.1). That dream came true and she was on maternity leave when I had this dream.

One day while still on maternity leave, Tara showed up to attend our regularly scheduled weekly staff meeting. She brought in her baby, so I thought that was why she came. During the staff meeting she said she had an important announcement to make. She then informed us that one of our project leads was promoted to a project manager and would be leaving to another group. It hit me then – my supervisor was still on maternity leave, but it was the project lead who was leaving the group. However, shortly after returning from maternity leave, she too moved to a different group, after first moving me out of the group on March 24, 2006.

(Dream 10.4, Sociable Co-worker, 02/06/2005, Jenness)

I am at my mother's home. I am looking for things to prepare for my daughter to go back to school.

After a while, I notice my co-worker, Don. He is with my nephew, John, who is giving him a tour of the property. Don is asking questions. He is talking to John in a friendly manner, which is typical of him. I get the feeling he is quite harmless and friendly. It feels like a family atmosphere.

God revealed to me that Don wouldn't be the person to force me out of my job position. I had this dream roughly two weeks after my sister, Ruth, dreamt about a person trying to force me out of the driver's seat while her boss was sitting in the front passenger's seat of a car.

After Ruth's dream, I was wondering if Don, who just got transferred into my group, was the one to which the dream applied. I did not have any reason to think he meant me any harm, but I just wondered. However, in about a week, the Lord chose to set my mind at ease with this co-worker.

From this dream, I learned not to ponder too much about my dreams, but to let things get revealed in time. I concluded that the Lord just showed me a few things here and there, so I would not worry when they happened. I consider myself to be blessed.

A few months after this dream an incident occurred, which identified the person who was trying to get my job position, according to Ruth's dream. After I got an assignment in which this person refused to give me all the information I needed to get the job done in a reasonable amount of time, I knew for sure to whom this dream applied. The person had expertise in that area. Because of the lack of information, I refused to even start the assignment; thereby assisting the person in achieving the set goal. I saw no reason to start something from scratch, which someone knew thoroughly; wasting time and company's money. After I got transferred to another group, the person to which this dream applied got hired in my former group.

(Dream 10.5, Lizard Skin, 7/20/2006, Jenness)

I am at a house that is unfamiliar to me. Don passes by with the skin of a lizard. It is green, very long, and about one inch in diameter. He says to me, "You want to see this?" He hangs it on a nail in the wall and then leaves.

Later, I am in another room of the same house with my daughter, Kristal. My supervisor, Sarah, comes by with the same lizard skin. She shoves it into my hands then walks away. Kristal sees it and gets upset. She says to me, "I don't like that." I take the lizard skin and tear it to pieces with my bare hands. I throw the pieces into the garbage. I am not afraid of it.

A few days after this dream, I discovered what the lizard skin was about. While testing software applications with two men in my group, Tom and Reenan, Tom had a fit just because I decided to check on the behavior of an application on one of the workstations and then report my findings to him. He was chosen to document the test results. He said, "*I didn't get to see that.*" Reenan usually observed the test result and then gave Tom the results to write up. I was new to the group but had learned the new procedures for that kind of testing and was well-established as a trustworthy tester in the other group, which they were both aware of.

For me, Tom used that opportunity to show me I was not wanted in the group. He threw down his pen in disgust; made some comments I couldn't hear; and then walked away with deliberate steps. Although I was new to the group, I felt I was qualified enough to make simple observations and report them, as did Reenan.

As we continued testing together later in the day, I saw Tom take my water bottle out of the way and throw it down hard on the bench while uttering something, which I did not hear. A teammate from another group, Taze, witnessed the action and when Tom walked out deliberately, once again, Taze asked, *"What was that all about?"* There were other incidences in which Tom deliberately reacted in a negative way towards me; making sure I saw his behavior. Tom, and not Don, as in the dream, was in no uncertain way showing me the *"lizard skin,"* again and again.

The following day, our project lead, Sarah, assigned me to do some other work while the other two teammates continued testing. My daughter, Krystal, called me about something she was upset with in her new job. I realize this was an element in this dream fulfillment. Krystal was also upset in the dream. She called me while she was upset and while other parts of the dream fulfillment were in progress.

The week following this dream, I had a performance review with Sarah. Our manager, David, also came along. Sarah went through each item I was rated on, by my peers as well as her. I was told I was doing things without telling my team members, etc. I was surprised I was given four poor ratings. Sarah's action was related to her showing the lizard skin to me in the dream, after Don (in real life, Tom) already showed it to me.

I told Sarah she shouldn't just listen to what one team member said. If there was a problem within the team, then there should be a team meeting where we could discuss it.

I was not afraid to speak up for myself, much like the way I was not afraid of the lizard skin in the dream. I handled the situation by pointing out I was just transferred from the other group where I had to coordinate complicated work assignments with other group members. In the previous group, we worked in such a way that the work could be handed off to the other team member, seamlessly. However, the members in her group did not seem to welcome me.

(Dream 10.6, Lining Up to Go, 12/15/2006, Jenness)

I am in a building that is supposed to be where I work. I see a paper with a long list of numbers and their meaning beside them. I stare for a while but can only focus on one of the numbers. I see that it has three digits. I cannot make out what the middle number is, but the beginning and ending numbers are both 7.

While I am looking at the numbers, a coworker says to me, "It means you can leave early if you want." I look and see a lot of people lining up to go. I get up to join the line. When I reach the end of the line, I see that it is too long. I get impatient and decide to go in the opposite direction of the line and onto a road. It is a well-paved road. I make a right turn on the road.

The dream scene changes. I find myself packing my lunch to go to work. Next, I am driving to work. The roads look all new. I come at a crossroad.

I look to my left and see the building where I will be working. The building looks new. It is a brick building. The bricks have the same color as the building where I currently work. I can see clearly on the building the word, WOT.

Some people started leaving the company after an announcement of organizational realignment. However, what was more interesting was the fact that later, while I was out on sick leave, I learned that three of my co-workers from my group resigned. The line of people leaving became a reality. Relative to the 7 and 7 as digits in the dream was the number of questions on our revised performance review measurement matrix, 77.

The day after the dream, we had a mandatory staff meeting at work. It was about a new system of measuring performance of employees. The project leader went through the process of explaining how to use the new system. I was surprised when she said, *"There are now seventy-seven questions."* We didn't have that many in the previous system of evaluation. At that moment, I remembered this dream. There were rumors going around about layoffs for the following year. Some had already occurred in another area of the company.

This dream is an outstanding example of how God works through dreams. At the time of this dream, I was working on a project, WAN Outage Testing, which was abbreviated as WOT. Much later, when I was deciding on a name for God's company, I was able to reverse engineer the abbreviation, WOT, to Works Of Trinity. God had shown me the name of His company, in this dream. The initial products of Works Of Trinity will be books written about my experiences with God, Jesus, and the Holy Spirit.

(Dream 10.7, Transferring to Georgia, 1/10/2007, Jenness)

I am at a place. There is a crowd of people. Dorothy Jenkins, the Portfolio Manager of my group, is having a meeting. It is the end of the meeting and people are moving away. I know she selected some people to be transferred to Georgia. I also know that Charles, Edwardo, and I are among the chosen. I am not sure of what the job would entail.

My husband is there with me. I say to him, "I don't know if I want to go to Georgia. I don't know if they will want me to work in production and I have back problems." I start to think, "Maybe this is a good time to do my own business." As I walk with my husband, we see a black man and his wife. The man calls my husband and shows him a picture of his wife and himself in a newspaper. He knows that my husband is in the real estate business and therefore he wants to talk to him.

Although the part about me moving to Georgia did not occur, my husband met a co-worker from my company at a real estate meeting and he was questioning my husband about real estate. During the conversation, my husband learned he was transferred from Georgia eight months ago. He was interested in real estate while in Georgia, so he decided to check it out in the area where he was living.

Another aspect of this dream came true in a relative way. In early April 2010, my current group was reassigned a female portfolio manager who worked out of Georgia. This was the same management level as Dorothy Jenkins in the dream. People in my current group started to wonder if we would be transferred to Georgia.

(Dream 10.8, Check My Clothes, 3/21/2007, Jenness)

I am at work. I see my supervisor, Sarah. She doesn't say anything to me. I don't say anything to her. I suddenly remember I have clothes in the dryer. I walk to where the dryer is located. I see two dryers, one stack on top of the other. I start to take my clothes from the top dryer.

Sarah comes in and starts to put her clothes in the bottom dryer. I take out all my clothes and start to fold them. They are all sheets. Sarah is there while I am folding my clothes. She doesn't say anything to me. I don't say anything to her.

This dream was fulfilled in a relative way. Relative to me paying attention to my clothes was the fact that in real life I had to start pay attention to how I dress before going to work.

The day following this dream, March 22, 2007, I went to work. I saw a document on my chair with the company's guidelines for dressing. It was opened to page 2 of 4. I saw T-shirts, sweatshirts, and Turtleneck, highlighted in yellow.

I saw that the document was printed from the company's internal website. It had the logon user name as one of the guys in my group, Tom. Later that day I asked Tom if he left a document on my chair. I did not specify the kind of document. He denied it. I figured that my supervisor did it because when I left work the previous day; Tom was usually gone by them. Furthermore, the previous day she had mentioned her computer was giving trouble. I figured she had asked Tom to print it out for her. I guessed she wanted the hint to be anonymous, but she didn't realize the document had Tom's name on it.

I did not mention anything to Sarah about the document on my chair because I realized she was trying to anonymously inform me to stop wearing T-shirt looking tops. However, I made a conscious effort when selecting clothes to wear to work, so that I could abide by the company's dress codes.

This dream confirms to me that although some people might feel comfortable with themselves, thinking they have accomplished something anonymously, they do not realize that God sees everything. He has His way of exposing things.

(Dream 10.9, He Has My Problem, 5/18/2007, Jenness)

I am at work. I am in a room. A tall man writes on the blackboard. He puts two column headings at the top of the board. A co-worker, Tom, is in the room.

After the man stops writing on the board, Tom goes up and writes. He starts his writing at the middle of the board. The man asks, "Why did you write so low?" Tom replies, "My hand and all the way down my back are stiff and hurting." He moves his right hand down his right side to emphasize what he is saying.

I say, "That's the kind of problem I have been having." I start to laugh. Tom gets upset and walks out. I say to myself, "I have to apologize to him."

This dream was fulfilled. Months later, I saw Tom walking one-sided at work. After that, he was out of work for a while, due to back problems.

****

The works of God through dreams started with outstanding dreams that caused me to pay attention to them. After God saw that dreams caught my attention, He started showing me things people were doing against me before they happened. God also started showing me when I was under spiritual attack. The works of God through dreams were not limited to myself, but extended to my family, friends, and co-workers. God showed me their situations before they became reality.

There is no limit to how God works through dreams. It was through a dream that He gave me the abbreviation that lead to His company's name. Through dreams, God called me to be His apostle and to do His mission. It was through a dream Jesus asked me to write books for Him. I knew they should be about my dreams and spiritual experiences.

Dreams are good, when they have a Divine connection. Those who love and trust God can be assured that dream is one way in which He communicates with them. There are many examples in the Bible.

Chapter 11
An Outstanding Biblical Dream

Biblical dreams are stories in the Bible that tell of God communicating with His children, while they are asleep. Some of these dreams, as in the book of Revelation, though not clear and direct, are classified as visions. They contain symbols of animals; such as dragon, beast, and serpent; and symbols of things, such as corn, field, moon, and star to depict the character of the person or situation when the dreams or visions are being fulfilled.

We were binding sheaves of grain in the field when my sheaf stood upright while your sheaves gathered around mine and bowed to it (Genesis 37:7).

In the dream above, God shared the big plans He had for Joseph's future. When Joseph shared his dream with his brothers they correctly interpreted it as the future reign of Joseph over them. Joseph's brothers' sheaves bowing down to his sheaf symbolized them bowing to him. Joseph's brothers despised him because of it and began to plot his death.

There are many dream experiences in the Bible, but I will focus on the dream stories of Joseph since I feel a special connection to his experiences. Joseph's life experiences are centered around his dreams and their fulfillments. These are told in Genesis chapters 37 to 45. I can relate to Joseph because God's plans for my future were also illustrated in dreams. Joseph's dreams are recorded in the Holy Bible and my dreams are recorded in books, mainly this one.

Joseph had another dream in which the sun, moon, and eleven stars bowed down to him (Genesis 37:9). This dream indicated that not only his eleven brothers would bow down to him, but also his father and mother. When this was told to his brothers, it stirred up worse envy. Joseph's father was also upset with this dream, since it implied that Joseph would rule not only over his brothers, but over him and his wife.

Because of the resentment Joseph's brothers had for his promised prosperous future, they threw him into a pit and later sold him into slavery. Joseph's brothers' scheme could not foil God's master plan for Joseph. God has a way of turning evil into good.

Joseph was later re-sold to Potiphar, an officer of Pharaoh, captain of the guard. This allowed Joseph to gain critical access to the household where his leadership abilities would be recognized. However, there were more hurdles ahead of Joseph. Soon he was thrown into jail because Potiphar's wife falsely accused him of rape.

Not to worry, even Joseph's second jail sentence was a part of God's plan to position him even more closely to the work God had planned for him. By interpreting the dreams of the Pharaoh's butler and baker, Joseph was able to get the attention of Pharaoh. Joseph was able to interpret Pharaoh's dreams when his magicians could not. Pharaoh realized that God was with Joseph and, therefore, made him ruler over his house, his people, and all the land of Egypt.

Joseph interpretation of Pharaoh's dream as a warning of a famine was the gateway to the fulfillment of his own dreams. The famine took place. However, Egypt was ready for it because Pharaoh heeded Joseph's dream interpretation and prepared for it. Joseph's father had to send his brothers twice to Egypt to get food for the family. Joseph's brothers and later his father had to humble themselves before him, thus fulfilling his dreams of them bowing to him.

There are many other examples of dream fulfilled in the Bible; some of which God gave warnings, gifts, and directions to people (Genesis 20; 31; I Kings 3; Matthew 1; 2). The number of dreams stories in the Bible clearly indicates that dreams are an important way in which God communicates with us.

Joseph's experiences teach us that the fulfillment of some of God's dreams can lead you through some very rough paths that you might think have nothing to do with God. Like Joseph, I have held on to the dreams that are clearly related to God's plan for me; despite the rocky road. I can't figure out God's plan exactly, but I know He has plans of prosperity for my future. I have experienced the fulfillment of His promises in many of my dreams. However, for some reason, I am still treading the rough road, which will lead to the Lord's deliverance.

Chapter 12
A Look at Biblical Dreams

The Biblical dreams that I have identified will help to bring home the point that dreams were reverenced in those days. People saw it as a way that God used to communicate with them. For those who did not understand the meanings of their dreams, they sought the help of interpreters.

The dream examples from the Holy Bible given here show where God used dreams to warn, reveal, direct, and give gifts.

In dreams, God warned:

- Abimelech about being married to another man's wife (Genesis 20:3-6)
- Laban against speaking to Jacob after he pursued and overtook Jacob (Genesis 31:24)
- The wise men not to return to Herod since God knew that Herod intended to kill Jesus (Matthew 2:11-12)

- Joseph to flee with Jesus to Egypt to prevent Him from getting killed by Heron's men (Matthew 2:13)
- Joseph about Archelaus who took over the reign of this father, Herod, so that Joseph would settle in Galilee rather than go back to Israel (Matthew 2:22)

Through dreams, God revealed:

- Joseph's future to him; in that, he would become ruler over his brothers and parents (Genesis 37:5-11)
- To Pharaoh's chief butler what would happen to him in the future (Genesis 40:8-11)
- To Pharaoh's baker what would happen to him in the future (Genesis 40:16-17)
- Victory in war to Gideon, through a man (Judges 7:13-15)
- The meaning of King Nebuchadnezzar's dream to Daniel after he prayed for its revelation (Daniel 2:19-45)
- To King Nebuchadnezzar what he would lose his kingdom and mind. He would become like a wild animal until he acknowledged God as the supreme ruler who takes away and

gives kingdoms to whomever He wants (Daniel 4:9-7).

- To Daniel the rule of four kings represented by the four beasts coming out of the sea, followed by the coming of the Son of man. This troubling dream caused Daniel to experience real feeling of grief during the dream (Daniel 7:1-28).

In dreams, God directed:

- Joseph to take Mary as his wife even though she was pregnant with God's son. Joseph had thoughts of quietly breaking off their engagement (Matthew 1:19-21).
- Joseph to go to Israel when it was safe for Jesus because Herod who sought to kill Him was dead (Matthew 2:19-20)

Through dreams, God gave:

- Pharaoh a vision of the future of his country with seven years of plenty followed by seven years of famine. Through Joseph's interpretation of the dream, Pharaoh was able to prepare his country for the time of famine (Genesis 41:15-27).

- The gift of Laban's cattle to Jacob through promised wages. This is after God saw the injustice being done to Jacob. Laban, his father-in-law, changed his wages ten times to pay him less in cattle for his labor (Genesis 31:10-12).
- The gift of wisdom, riches, and honor to Solomon. This was after God saw that Solomon loved and worshipped Him with sacrifices in high places. God granted Solomon the desire of his heart (I Kings 3:5-15).

Real feelings can be experienced in dreams as when Daniel experienced the real feeling of grief about the four beasts (Daniel 7:1-28). I can relate to Daniels feelings in dreams since I often get the feeling of reality while dreaming.

Also, gifts from God can come through dreams. He gave the gift of His herb through a dream like when He gave Solomon the gift of wisdom, riches, and honor and Laban's cattle to Jacob (I Kings 3:5-15; Genesis 31:10-12).

Chapter 13

Summary

This book has taken you on my dream journey. There are a few dreams from close relatives, which relate to the same situation in the dream stories. It was the realization of my many dream fulfillments and the request of Jesus Christ to write books for Him that propelled me to write this book. In 2006 to 2007, I did a draft of this book, had it partially edited, and then put it aside.

On January 10, 2010, I experienced an encounter with Jesus in which I promised Him to write His books. I know that this dream book is one of those that are commissioned by Him to be written about my life experiences in which He was deeply involved.

It is necessary that this book precede the second book since it is about incidents which these many dreams prepared my family and me to face. The second book Jesus commissioned me to write is, *God's Mission: Spiritual Battles and Revelation of Anti-666*. Later, the story of God leading me to establish His business is written in my book, *God Has Gone Corporate*. In all these books, I must give honor to Jesus Christ of Nazareth for providing me with the stories to write the books, so that I can keep my promise of writing books for Him.

Bibliography

Delaney, Gayle, Ph. D. *All About Dreams: Everything You Need To know About *Why We Have Them *What They Mean *and How To Put Them To Work for You.* New York, NY: HarperCollins Publishers Inc, 1998.

"dream." *Merriam-Webster.com.* Merriam-Webster, 2012. Web. 4 January 2012.

Fishman, Gary. *Dream Interpretation.* Manahawkin, NJ: Waymaker Media, 2016.

Mcafee, Tierney. "Trump Flubs Anti-Abortion Speech: It's 'Wrong' for Babies to Be 'Born' in Ninth Month." *People Politics.* 19 January 2018. Web. Accessed 28 January 2018.

Miller, Gustavus Hindman. *10,000 Dreams Interpreted: A Dictionary of Dreams.* Simon & Schuster. 1984.

PubMed Health. *Sarcoidosis.* http://www.ncbi.nlm.nih.gov/pubmedhealth/PMH0001140/. Accessed 11 November 2009.

Reverend Yong Gyu, Park. *Heaven & Hell 1000 to 1.* http:// www.spiritlessons.com/Documents/Pastor_Park/index.htm. Accessed 23February 2012.

Robinson, Stearn and Gorbett, Tom. *The Dreamer's Dictionary: From A to Z... 3000 Magical Mirrors to Reveal the Meaning of Your Dreams.* Warner Books. 1975.

Rodriguez, Janet. *Let the Truth Be Told.* Xulon Press, 2011.

The Holy Bible. King James Version. Holman Bible Publishers, 1979.

Tortello, R., Ph. D. "Jamaican Folk Customs and Superstitions, SUPERSTITIONS." *The Gleaner*, 2007.Accessed 30 June 2010. http://www.jamaica-gleaner.com/gleaner/20070806/lead/lead5.html.

Vanderhee, Kimbella. Interview with Scott-Young, Mona. *Love & Hip Hop: The best moments from reality check. TV.* VH1. 6 February 2012.

www.ingramcontent.com/pod-product-compliance
Lightning Source LLC
Chambersburg PA
CBHW020650300426
44112CB00007B/320